HOW TO
GROW OLD

JOHN BISHOP

HOW TO GROW OLD

EBURY
PRESS

1 3 5 7 9 10 8 6 4 2

Ebury Press, an imprint of Ebury Publishing
20 Vauxhall Bridge Road
London SW1V 2SA

Ebury Press is part of the Penguin Random House group of companies
whose addresses can be found at global.penguinrandomhouse.com

Penguin
Random House
UK

First published by Ebury Press in 2019
This edition published 2020

www.penguin.co.uk

A CIP catalogue record for this book is available from the British Library

ISBN 9781529105421

Typeset in 9.39 pt/15.2 pt ITC Galliard Pro
by Integra Software Services Pvt. Ltd, Pondicherry

Printed and bound in Great Britain by Clays Ltd, Elcograf S.p.A.

Penguin Random House is committed to a
sustainable future for our business, our readers
and our planet. This book is made from Forest
Stewardship Council® certified paper.

I would like to dedicate this to the older people in my life, who are important to me every day.

Ernie and Kathleen Bishop, my mum and dad. I would not exist without them and I would not be a fraction of the man I am had they not been my parents. I love them more than I can ever say. Mike Cornall, Melanie's father, whose sharp mind and quick wit I have always appreciated. I learn from him every time we speak. Eileen Garnett, Melanie's mother, who we lost as I was starting this book. Not many people have a mother-in-law as a friend. I did. We miss her dearly. She would have loved this.

CONTENTS

Introduction   ix

1. How to Wake Up Old   1

2. How to Dress   21

3. How to Be a Family Man   63

4. How to Be a Friend   81

5. How to Still Be Funny   107

6. How to Go on Holiday   123

7. How to Stay Fit and Still Love Sport   139

8. How to Stay Relevant   187

9. How to End This Book   217

Acknowledgements   233

INTRODUCTION

WHEN I DEVELOP A new stand-up tour, I tend to start from nothing. Some comedians carry a notebook around ready to pounce on anything that happens or is said, and which may be developed into 'a bit' – a bit being the universal comedians' name for a piece of stand-up material. I have never operated like that, primarily because I came to comedy late and was too busy working and bringing up kids to be thinking what part of my life I could use on stage. I would go on stage, see what bits sprang to mind, and expand those themes further in subsequent gigs.

This is fine when you are doing ten-minute spots in comedy clubs. But when it comes to putting together a tour that needs two hours of new material, I often wish I had the discipline of noting down any bits that have happened. Essentially, I am not a joke-teller. When I am on stage, I talk about what has happened in my world: my life, therefore, is spent walking around, hoping that something funny happens. When something humorous *does* occur, I retell it on stage to a room full of strangers – as long as

I can remember it, of course. As I have now reached the stage in my life where I can't always remember what I did yesterday, that isn't guaranteed.

Having no notebooks to start from, I basically do tons of smaller warm-up shows, where I always seem to find the main things that are playing on my mind at that point in my life. It's a bit like therapy, as it helps organise my mind, if therapy consisted of standing in front of a room of unqualified people who I have asked to pay to attend. The process starts with standard room-above-a-pub gigs, moves onto small art centres with a few hundred people, and steadily grows in venue size as I develop the material into a full show.

I like this process more than if I prepared – or you could say, if I acted more professionally! I know it's counter-intuitive, but the less preparation I have for those early warm-up gigs, the better the overall end result is when I develop the full show. In the absence of any prepared material to fall back on, I find I am forced to allow the adrenaline to kick in and stimulate the creative process. Nothing activates your brain more than standing in front of a room full of strangers looking at you with expectant faces, waiting for you to be funny while all you have to offer is a blank mind and a microphone. I seem to find the material quicker in those situations than I do sat at home looking at the wall with a blank page and a pen.

This approach also means the material is more 'of the moment'. It is based on the stuff that is currently happening or currently in my head, which makes it feel fresh and relevant. On my last tour, *Winging It*, two main things kept informing the material. Firstly, I had just turned fifty, and secondly, my kids had left home (by choice, I might add: we didn't just kick them out so I would have some material for the show, although I would probably have felt it was a price worth paying in the absence of any other bits).

When this book's publisher, Andrew, watched the DVD of the show, he reported back that it was basically 'a middle-aged man moaning'. However, this was much more of a positive than a negative, as he said there was a market for this as a book: many people were probably feeling the same, and Andrew suggested this could be used as a reference point for anyone in a similar position or about to face the same challenges. It was his suggestion to call this book *How to Grow Old*. It was my later suggestion to add the subtitle, *A Middle-Aged Man Moaning*.

I am now sat at home, tapping away at this introduction with the three-finger style I have developed as I never thought typing was going to be a skill I would ever require. I am part of the generation of men born in a time when only secretaries, journalists and authors knew how to type. Email, the creation of which has revolutionised communication, was not even invented when I entered the adult world of work, aged sixteen.

My first full-time job was as a mail lad (there were no mail girls, or mail persons of gender neutrality, in 1982) and my role entailed cycling around the ICI Rocksavage chemical plant in Runcorn, taking handwritten notes between the offices and plant rooms. The company sent its products all over the world and was regarded as the cutting-edge of technology, but could only operate because sixteen-year-old mail lads on bikes carried notes in brown envelopes between all the people involved in the production process.

ICI was regarded as a great employer, and often the old men I would see walking around the yard in company overalls and hard hats would tell me to stick with the company because I would get my pension, provided I progressed from the mail room and learned one of the skills the company required, such as operating some of the plant machinery. Nobody ever said to me, 'Listen, son, learn to type! It's the future and will change your life. It will save you from looking like a man with arthritis who can only use three fingers, when you're fifty-two.'

Nobody ever said that because the office environment in those days really was 'paper shuffling'. Today, I would imagine that the offices in ICI are filled with people on laptops typing away and communicating with the world instantly through their fingertips. Back in 1982, the phones had rotary dials on the front which meant even dialling a call would take five minutes. All written communication was on memo pads that had a space for the next person to respond to what was written in the box above, and to stimulate the next person in line to engage. What would now be done with a single group email would take days, as notes were carried from one part of the plant to another.

Part of me misses those times, because the frenetic speed we operate and communicate at nowadays doesn't seem to have served us very well. Everyone is stressed and overloaded with information, and email means that you are never really away from work. It is too easy to be on a family holiday and let the 'I just have to deal with this one email' mentality creep in. Even if it is only thirty minutes away from the family holiday, it is still time lost you will never get back.

That never happened when I was a mail lad. Nobody ever said, 'John, take this memo to Keith from accounts. He is in Malaga with his family, but if you can just cycle there, and wait an hour for him to read it and respond and bring it back, that would be great.'

Not only would that have killed me on my fixed-wheel butcher's bike with my mail bag in the front basket, but Keith would almost certainly have said, 'Fuck off! I'm on holiday!'

These days, someone would just 'ping' Keith an email and either through a sense of responsibility or a fear of being sacked (or to get away from his annoying family), Keith would find a quiet corner, read the email and type a response. Most of us do this without thinking about it, even though logic suggests it is an intrusion we should object to. And that's despite the fact that many people's typing skills, particularly people under the age of thirty, now mean they can communicate with their fingers quicker than their mouth – as any parent who has ever had a text argument with a teenager will testify. I have done that with my sons and it's quite disconcerting when they reply to a text you have not yet finished typing.

Typing for me is like talking with a speech impediment: I can make myself understood but it takes me longer than I would like. The difference is that if I had a speech impediment (accents don't count!), I would seek help, but one sign of aging is the acceptance that this is as good as you will ever be at something. Don't believe people who take on new hobbies in their later years and pretend they are doing it as part of some journey of self-development. They just can't be arsed getting better at the things they already do.

How to Grow Old is a stupid title, because the answer is obvious: *Don't Die.* Provided you don't die, you are growing old. You are already older than when you started reading this book, and that was only a few minutes ago.

In fact, getting old is not that difficult in the modern western world. Life expectancy has increased dramatically. Women's life expectancy in the UK today is 82.9 years, and for men 79.2 years:

back in 1841, it was 42.2 and 40.2, which means it has virtually doubled. No other creature in the whole history of the planet has managed to affect its own life expectancy in such a positive way and in such a relatively short space of time. If anything, the life expectancy of many animals on Earth has been adversely affected by the extension of ours: the longer we live, the more resources we will use.

Whichever way you look at it, a doubling of human life expectancy in only 178 years is incredible. There are many factors that have influenced this, and some we will pick up further in the book, but if the same thing happened again in the next 178 years, then in 2197 we could be expecting an average life expectancy of 160 years old. It will be like living in a world of Gandalfs, but it may well happen. Since the 1980s, life expectancy has continued to go up by around two months a year because of fewer deaths from smoking or heart problems, thanks to healthier lifestyles and better health care.

However, the length of time you can expect to be on this planet may be predetermined before you even get here. Where you come from defines how long you live more than most people would imagine. In 2017, the Office of National Statistics found males living in the most affluent 10 per cent of areas in England and Wales lived an average 9.3 years longer than males living in the bottom 10 per cent. Life expectancy is longer in the South than the North or the Midlands: kids born between 2010 and 2012 could expect to live an average of 80.3 years in the South East and 79.7 in London, but only 77.8 in the North East and 77.7 in the North West.

This difference becomes more distinct between areas and even postcodes. Men born in Kensington live a decade longer than men born in Glasgow (73). However, this difference is outdone by that of the men living in Warfield Harvest Ride, in Berkshire, who can expect to live until 90.3, and men living in the Bloomfield area of Blackpool who live to an average 68.2. That's a staggering 22.1 years' difference between two places in the same country that are about 240 miles apart – nearly a year of extra life for every 11 miles.*

As shocking as this statistic is, I hope you haven't bought this book called *How to Grow Old* looking for the answer. If you live in Bloomfield and are thinking, 'That's good, I could buy that book, read it and learn from the wisdom within its pages, and then I too can live as long as the people in Warfield Harvest Ride ...' then I'm afraid you're going to be disappointed. It is also worth pointing out that these statistics assume that where you are born or where you spend most of your life does not change. There is nothing in the genetic make-up of the people of Kensington that guarantees longevity. Should a child be taken from the environment of Kensington or Warfield Harvest Ride and placed in Bloomfield or Glasgow to grow up, one would suspect they would not outlive their new peers. In fact, arriving in Glasgow with a clipped, posh Berkshire accent? It's fair to say your chances of longevity will be massively curtailed.

Living longer doesn't always mean having a better life. It's not as if the people in Warfield Harvest Ride have a longer period of life in their twenties and thirties, when they are fit, with tight stomachs and boundless energy which they can direct into having more sex, doing more travelling and learning new skills – which in turn leads to them meeting new people they can travel with, learn

---

* *I have no information about how many men actually live in these two areas. There may only be one man in each place, and if one is a chain-smoking alcoholic and the other a geriatric yoga guru, then there is a decent chance you get these results. As I have no intention of going to either place to investigate, let's just all agree it does seem unfair and a further illustration of how divided we are as a nation.*

new skills with and have more sex with. It's not as if they gain more time in the best years of their lives.

No, the people in Warfield Harvest Ride gain more time at the fag-end of their life. They have more time when they don't understand the changing world, when less people are bothered about what they think, and when their only contribution to society is to carry on living to get statisticians excited. The older you live, the more time you spend in a body that is not what you ever thought it would be, looking at yourself in the mirror and remembering when all your skin used to fit your face instead of the saggy bag with eyes looking back at you.

This book will not tell you how to stay on this planet longer. Instead, it will attempt to look at the various aspects of being the age I am today – fifty-two, at time of writing – that make me see the world differently, and to share some of the things I have learned along the way. Some of it will be funny, hopefully, some will involve genuine lessons from my life, and some of it will contain elements that, as I sit here typing the first pages, I can't anticipate.

I also need to point out that I am a white, heterosexual, middle-aged man: the exact demographic from whom the world no longer wants to learn anything. I am very aware that nobody is having marches for white, heterosexual, middle-aged men. There is no drive to ensure that we are we represented equally on television and in the media. Nobody is speaking up for us because we have had the patriarchal society for millennia, most people think we've made a bollocks of it and so now it's someone else's turn.

This is not a complaint but an observation. Straight white middle-aged men have had our time and so it's only fair we hear some other voices. I only mention this here as a spoiler alert: I can only see the world through the eyes of my own experience and that will become more apparent through these pages.

Andrew, my publisher, is a white, heterosexual middle-aged man himself, so when he approached me to write this book, I knew I had probably struck a chord with him through my stand-up. As I am not a professional writer, Andrew thought it would make sense to link me up with an experienced writer and editor, and so introduced me to Ian Gittins. Ian has been very hands-on and the fact that this book exists at all is in no small measure down to him. He has given me feedback on what I have written, and suggested edits and other topics to explore. When I was halfway through the book and sent him an email with the subject title 'I can't be arsed ...' explaining that as a grumpy middle-aged man I was losing the will to live, or at least losing the will to try and fill any of the empty pages that were in front of me, he suggested we could keep moving things forward by finding other ways to get the material of the book down. Ian came to my house and recorded conversations we had, that he then wrote up and returned to me to use as I wished. This was an interesting process akin to developing a stand-up tour because I could read and reflect on what we had discussed and extract material to change or rewrite to include in the book. It kept my brain engaged when I had reached the conclusion that wasting my life writing a book about growing old was more irony that even I could stand.

As another white, heterosexual middle-aged man, Ian brought absolutely nothing new to the demographic of the team working on this book. Normally, if three white, heterosexual middle-aged men are working to put something on paper it is either government legislation, a fantasy football league or a pub quiz. Hopefully, this book will fill a gap in-between.

Basically, if you want to know how to grow old, I am not sure this book will help. If you want to understand the aging process from a sociological and anthropological perspective, I am not sure it will do that, either. However, if you happen to want to know what white, heterosexual, middle-aged men think of getting old, this book could very well be exactly what you have been looking for.

1.
HOW TO WAKE UP OLD

HOW DO YOU KNOW you are officially 'old'? I think there is a very easy way to find out. Take your current age and halve it. If the person you were half a lifetime ago was still at school, you're not old. If the person you were half a lifetime ago was, even then, grown up enough to have a job with a pension plan and a company car, as I was twenty-six years ago, then you are old. I do this exercise from time to time: pause and try to remember what stage I was at in my life ten, twenty or, in this case, twenty-six years ago. It's an exercise which is always filled with both joy and sadness. Joy that the Me I was then would be pleased to see Me as I am today; sadness that I didn't appreciate my life then enough.

The old cliché that 'You are only as old as you feel' always sounds great. It's optimistic and suggests that your age is up to you: think positively and your age will be what you want it to be. Some people think that this is all that matters, how young you feel. Emile Ratelband, a Dutch TV personality, felt so strongly about it that he took legal action to get his age of sixty-nine reduced to forty-nine, to reflect more how he felt but also to help with his profile on dating websites. He argued that if he felt forty-nine he should be able to say he was forty-nine, in the same way that transgender people can change their sex legally. Life, however, is not an internet dating profile and he lost the case because the judges suggested it would open the law up to all sorts of abuse, because if people could reduce their age legally they could also increase it to break age restrictions to marry, drink alcohol or even vote. He also lost the case because it was a stupid thing to take to a court of law: you can't just *decide* to be a different age, and there is not a direct correlation between actual legal age and how you feel. That would be like going to court and asking them to say you are taller and slimmer because you don't feel small and fat. Comparing it to the experience of the transgender community is a staggering display of ignorance. It's like coming back from holiday with a tan and saying you now know what it feels like to be black.

As you get older, everything about your life changes – including how you wake up. Waking up old is not the same as waking up young. When you are young, you bounce out of bed, do a few press-ups, and take your naked body to the shower to start the day. When you are old, you don't even wake up naked. Somehow, on the journey to becoming older, there is a point in your relationship with your partner where sleeping *au naturel* seems completely unnecessary. The idea that you might just happen to have passionate sex accidentally – and so need to keep that option open – is not realistic after a certain age.

You and your partner accept that you are going to bed to rest, not to engage in the acrobatics that being under a duvet together used to entail. It makes sense to be as comfortable as possible, which generally does not include being naked. Instead, you might wear an old T-shirt, or some official pyjamas. By 'official', I mean the

2

full matching patterned Marks & Spencer outfit, because for years I used to opt for just a T-shirt. That seemed fine until about five years ago, when my wife, Melanie, suggested I start to wear bed-pants.

Bed-pants are not pyjamas. They perform the same function of covering all the unacceptable parts of your body which gravity is doing its best to pull towards your ankles, but they are more like a cotton pair of shorts. In many quarters they appear cool, more like house shorts, or chill-out shorts to wear in front of the TV. Once you call them bed-pants, I realise, it sounds like I am going to bed in a nappy. I am not. I am going to bed in thigh-length cotton shorts that allow my wife to sleep in the knowledge that, should she kick the covers off to cool off during the night, she is not going to wake up and find she has my testicles stuck to her back.

How a couple undress for bed changes as they age. At the start of the relationship, you are driven by the desire to get your clothes off and jump into bed to have sex. In middle age, you have reached the stage where you can both get undressed in the same room and, once naked, start getting dressed again to go to bed. You are entering into a contract with each other, a contract that says, 'You and I have agreed that tonight is about sleep, and all that other smutty stuff will just have to wait its turn.'

This may sound sad on one level, but it's actually one of the most reassuring aspects about growing older together. Today, I could not imagine myself with a woman in her twenties, full of lust and adventure, lying on the bed in the best erotic outfit Ann Summers can offer, while I put on a T-shirt I wore on holiday three years ago and climb into my bed-pants. I think one of us would be severely disappointed.

One aspect about sharing space with another person is the acceptance of each other's morning ablutions. I remember reading Gabriel García Márquez's *Love in the Time of Cholera*, in which he magically captured the intimacy of a relationship through the partners feeling comfortable having a pee in front of each other. I am not talking about in a kinky, golden showers sort of way. I am talking about, 'I need a pee, and you know me so well I am not going to be embarrassed doing it in front of you, or you doing it in front of me.'*

In a relationship, you start out being icons to each other – as perfect as you can be, like two pristine Michelangelo statutes. Then the reality sets in and you stop thinking of poise and grace: you just become who you are, less something to wonder at like a statue but more something you would use every day, like a Hoover. There are, however, limits. I interviewed Miriam Margolyes a while ago. She was seventy-six at the time, and I asked her what she liked the most about growing old. She said, 'Taking time to enjoy a good shit.' It wasn't the answer I was expecting, but it was very funny. And it is true.

My interview with Miriam was for my *In Conversation With* … series on the W channel. I have interviewed quite a few older guests and they were all still extremely busy. That was definitely a good tip about getting older that I took from all of them: that you need to keep working, keep producing and keep being active, because then you will stay involved with life.

As you grow older, you become more aware of which of your achievements you should be most proud, and if I can digress for a second, I would say without doubt that my *In Conversation With* … series is the best thing I have ever done on television. It was just me and an interviewee for an hour at a time, and I loved it. Any

---

* *It's possible that Gabriel García Márquez expressed that thought somewhat better than I just did. He certainly never mentioned golden showers.*

TV host would be proud of the list of guests I talked to over four series. If you don't mind me being self-indulgent for a moment, I am going to list all of the guests I talked to, just for people who never saw or have never heard of the series.

Over four series of doing *In Conversation With . . .*, I spoke to James Corden, Charlotte Church, Steve Coogan, Alex Brooker, Kirsty Young, Freddie Flintoff, Lenny Henry, Jo Brand, Rupert Everett, Miriam Margolyes, Lindsay Lohan, Olly Murs, Louise Redknapp, Russell Brand, Ken Loach, Davina McCall, Ellie Simmonds, Jason Manford, Meera Syal, Anna Friel, David Walliams, Nadiya Hussain, Jimmy Carr, Craig Charles, Melanie C, John Cleese, Katie Price, Sam Womack, Dame Joan Collins, Professor Brian Cox, Professor Green, Ruth Jones, Paddy McGuinness, Katherine Ryan, Brendan Cole, Will Young, Cuba Gooding Jr, Alesha Dixon, Gabby Logan, Martine McCutcheon and Jeremy Corbyn.*

The programme was an interview show rather than a chat show. None of the guests came on because they were plugging anything: they came on simply because I thought they had a story and would be interesting to talk to for an hour. They certainly were.

As a side note, the show sadly became a victim of its own success. In order for W to film the show, I had to agree that over the next seven years they could repeat any episode twenty times. It meant that, in essence, we reached a tipping point after we had

---

* *Interestingly, of all of those stars of stage, screen and sport, the only interview that all three of my lads wanted to come to was Jeremy Corbyn. And they all wanted a photograph with him at the end. That must tell you something: Jeremy Corbyn is a grandad who has got an allotment and rides a bike, and yet he clearly had an appeal to young people (that was eighteen months ago though, and politics like showbusiness can change very quickly).*

recorded forty-one shows in two years: giving W forty-one shows to use twenty times each over the next seven years equated to 820 shows. It meant we came to a point where W simply didn't feel they needed any more interviews and, also, I felt the guests deserved to tell their stories to bigger audiences than W tended to get. However, if you haven't watched any of the shows, please do, or seek out the podcast version of the shows. I would stand by any episode, which is not something you can often say in the world of television.

At the time that I was doing those interviews, I had no idea that I would soon be writing this book about how to grow old. However, each of my more senior guests gave me some valuable nuggets of wisdom on the topic.

John Cleese has spent a few years waking up old by now. He was one of the people who said you have to keep moving and taking on new projects. As a comedy legend, he could have demanded anything from us, but all he asked for was thirty minutes peace and quiet so he could have a nap before make-up (he had been filming all day and he wore his slippers for the interview). I found him a joy to talk to: interesting, warm, funny and with many more layers to him than I initially thought.

Dame Joan Collins told me that she finds aging to be a strange process as she still feels young inside. She was eighty-four when I interviewed her and still had the bright eyes of a teenager. Her tips for growing older included not getting too skinny: being thin is what you aim for when you are young, she said, but as you get old, it makes you look weak and frail.*

---

* *I very much enjoyed being told by somebody who has lived through the most glamorous time in Hollywood, and who has been a sex symbol for decades, that it is OK to put on a bit of timber.*

Dame Joan was sharp, witty and a great example of the generation where stoicism and pride carried you through the tough times. She has certainly experienced some difficult periods and yet, like the old saying about the swan on the lake, nobody sees the hard work beneath the water as she glides serenely across the surface.

Despite being eighty when I talked to him, Ken Loach was also still incredibly busy. He had just released *I, Daniel Blake*, and after our interview was heading off to a community hall somewhere in London for a showing of the movie to people who worked in food banks. Ken said the most important thing about aging was to stick to your principles and have a cause and a reason to carry on. For Ken, social injustice drove him: not accolades and certainly not money or fame. As somebody who knows how seductive those two distractions can be, I greatly admire his choices.

This Is the Shit

But let's go back to Miriam Margoyles's pearl of wisdom about loving a 'good shit'. As I have grown older, I am also in less of rush when I go to the loo. In fact, I have found a pleasure in taking a dump that I could never have anticipated in earlier years.

I think it started to happen when the kids were young and the toilet became a sanctuary of calm and quiet. It was a haven where, for a few moments, you could be alone with your thoughts while the mayhem on the other side of the door was kept at bay by a tiny lock. Now the children have grown up and moved out, however, my relationship with Mr Crapper's gift to the world has evolved into one of a deeper understanding. The toilet is now a place where I can allow my body to catch up with itself and my mind can turn off all the multiple distractions that bombard it constantly during the day. I have even made a pact with myself to go to the toilet and leave my mobile phone outside (this only works at home: it's not a very sensible thing to do in a public convenience). Anyone who has ever answered the phone sat on a toilet knows the awkwardness of the question, 'So, what are you up to at the minute?'

My toilet at home has a magazine stand filled with copies of *National Geographic* magazine. I find it oddly reassuring to sit reading articles about the early humans and the division between *Homo sapiens* and Neanderthals while doing an activity that they too would have carried out. Admittedly, they would not have done so while perched on top of a porcelain throne, but at least while I poo I can sense some connection between myself and my primitive ancestors.

Allowing myself to take time over my dumps has also definitely increased my output. Not to put too fine a point on it, I am better at doing a dump now than at any time in my life – so much so that I class it as exercise. I even have proof of the benefits of this, and Melanie is a witness (not to the poo but to the facts). I weigh more than I look like I should. I always have done, and I genuinely have got big bones: I had a full body scan a few years ago which revealed I had the heaviest skeleton the radiologist had ever seen. These big bones are my excuse for being a slow runner, a slow walker, a slow cyclist and a heavy lover: fifteen stone of excitement is a lot for anyone to have on top of them (even if it is only for a couple of minutes). It's also why scales are not my friend, because I am always heavy.

For the last few years, my weight has fluctuated between 94 and 100 kilograms, which is basically 15 stone. When I was at my fittest, I was 13.5 stone, or 85 kilos. I will never see those days again and I am fine with that, as long as I have more muscle mass than fat. If I ever got to 14 stone, or about 90kg, that would be an achievement, but it would mean giving up many of the things I enjoy, such as red wine, and I am not sure I can be bothered. I exercise enough to remain healthy and that is the point. Even my youngest son, Daniel, recently told me, 'There is no way you should be that fat with all the exercise you do.' I *think* there was a compliment in there somewhere.

When I was going through one of my obsessive phases of trying to lose weight, we had a digital scale in our bathroom. I stood on it one morning and weighed 96.7kg. This was more than I had hoped for, so I put my kit on to go to the gym. Before I went, I had a coffee with Melanie and revealed my weight gain as if I was in a priest's confessional. I hoped she would forgive me with a few Hail Marys and I could avoid the gym. That didn't happen, but she did suggest I drink the coffee, take a dump and weigh myself again. I did so and now I weighed 95.2kg. I had just taken a 1.5kg dump. That is one-and-a-half bags of sugar, twenty-nine Mars bars, or fifty-three slices of bread. There have been babies born who weigh less than that. I couldn't believe it. There is no way I could expect to shift that much weight doing a session at the gym so, in celebration, I took my gym kit off and went out for a fry-up.

Every morning when I wake up old, I feel a mixture of joy, surprise and apprehension. The joy is there because, as a person, I am generally optimistic and have grown to love the fact that I wake up earlier than most people. I have never been somebody to lie in bed, an inability which used to really annoy me. I put this tendency down to my working-class genes, going back centuries, which have left me with the DNA of an eighteenth-century peasant farmer. This means that as soon I wake up, I feel I have to get up and start doing something to repay the tithes I owe to the landlord who rules the estate, and whose house I will one day burn down when I organise the other serfs and we take our pitchforks and claim back our rights. This is all a huge burden to have ingrained in my DNA particularly as I don't have a landlord to attack and nobody else is awake to start the revolution. However, it makes for a satisfying explanation as to why I don't lie in bed in the morning: it's because I need to be ready for the revolution.

This revolutionary gene appears to have stopped with me in my family, because my children show no interest in getting up early whatsoever. Being the father of sons, it was no surprise to me when their teenage years saw them lying in bed all morning. However, when they reached their twenties, I was expecting a change. Instead, when the boys come to visit now, Melanie reckons they are not coming to see us but returning for a cheap spa weekend. They spend most of the time in their bathrobes or pyjamas, get up some time in the afternoon, relax, eat some decent fresh food and disappear again.

As people get older, they generally need less sleep. The fact that I am writing this chapter of my book at 5.32am is testament to that fact. You know your life has changed from your mad twenties into your knackered fifties when you wake up at the same time that you used to come home. I'm not alone in needing less kip as the years go by. A survey in America by the National Sleep Foundation found that while infants should get 12–15 hours of Zzzs per day, and teenagers need 8–10 hours, middle-aged and older adults can easily get by with just seven. Sometimes they may not even get that as, for reasons that nobody is totally sure about, as we get older, we find it a lot harder to fall asleep. Perhaps our unconscious knows that the long sleep of death is getting closer, so we should not waste time sleeping now.

I think as you grow older you value your sleep more, particularly if you can split the day with the magic of an afternoon nap. This is something I think we need to make compulsory because it's like having two days in one. You spend the morning and early afternoon doing all the things you *have* to do. Then, after a nap, you can spend the late afternoon and evening doing all the things you *want* to do.

The Spanish are famous for their siestas, which began in rural communities as a practical way to deal with the searing midday heat. It was common sense that staying out of the sun when it was at its hottest would allow the workers to be more productive throughout the entire day. They worked a split day, taking a rest after lunch and working later into the evening. This lifestyle also matches the natural circadian rhythms that have been identified by scientists. Most human beings feel a dip in energy between 1 and 3pm but sadly in most of the industrialised world, bosses would frown on you hanging a hammock in your place of work. The British moved to industrialisation quicker than anyone and it was the industrialists of the eighteenth and nineteenth centuries who created the working day as we now know it. There again, back then working nine-to-five was considered part-time, and going home with all of your fingers intact showed a distinct lack of commitment to the company cause.

One of the biggest joys when I go on tour is my justified afternoon pre-show sleep. Being on tour means there is one single point in the day when I have to be at my best, and the rest of the day simply doesn't matter. As long as I am on stage at 8pm and say funny things for the following two hours, I am not judged by what else goes on in the day. This is incredibly liberating for someone with my personality and work ethic, where I intrinsically think I have to be doing something all of the time or I am either a) going to miss out or b) cheating, and wasting my day.

The practicalities of touring mean that I do a lot of travelling, and more preparation goes on behind the scenes than people would expect. Happily for me, the majority of that is done by other people. All that I have to do is turn up, do a soundcheck, get dressed and go on stage. If I'm playing a theatre, the sound-check can happen just before the doors open, but in an arena it's normally done around 4pm, which is perfect. I will head off to catering to have something to eat, then I'll go to a spare dressing room in the venue (there are always loads, as I am the only person on the night who needs one) and sleep on a blow-up bed. Or when I am not in too much of a rush, I'll go back to my hotel, get into a proper bed and kip. On tour, I always sleep for forty-five to sixty minutes at some point between four and seven.

An afternoon sleep is the single biggest determining factor affecting a gig for me. People often ask me if the audiences around the country differ, and if it is massively different doing an arena show to 10,000 people compared to a small theatre with 500? The answer is no, not really. What makes the most difference is whether I've had a kip.

There are venues where the response may be better due to the architecture of the venue: a Victorian theatre built for the spoken word will always have a better feel than an arena that spends half its time as an ice-skating ring. That's all to do with acoustics and atmosphere. There are also venues that, as a performer, will feel special to you. For me, it's the Liverpool Empire, where I recorded my first DVD: the Royal Albert Hall, because I could not believe I was doing sold-out one-man shows and standing on the stage where legends like Frank Sinatra had stood; and the 3 Arena in Dublin, partly because it's Dublin, and partly because it was one of the first arenas built in an amphitheatre style that makes even a huge gig feel intimate. I also have an affection for the Sydney Opera House because it is so iconic: to walk on stage there when they had oversold tickets to the extent that some of the audience were behind me was surreal to say the least.

I could easily list more venues and favourite cities, because I have great affection for many around the country, but the reality is that I have never found much of a correlation between geography and an audience laughing. In my experience if you are funny, they laugh; if you are not funny, they don't. Nobody arrives at a venue and decides that what they used to find funny is no longer funny or what they found to be unfunny is now hilarious. Laughter is too instinctive and spontaneous for that.

From my perspective, the size of the audience makes very little difference. Making 500 people laugh feels just as good as making 10,000 (although obviously that is assuming there are only 500 people in the room: only making 500 people out of 10,000 laugh would not be great). What I am trying to say is that the size of venue does not matter. I genuinely get the same level of enjoyment from all sizes of audiences. The two things that *do* matter are getting some sleep ... and the day of the week.

I do all that I can when I am on tour to avoid playing shows on Mondays. Nobody wants to laugh on a Monday. Years on the road have taught me that squeezing one extra night into the schedule is never a good idea if the extra night is a Monday. I would guess that at least 75 per cent of the audience buy the tickets so far in advance that they don't even realise it is a Monday. You walk on stage knowing that they looked at the tickets the week before, and stood in their kitchen saying 'Oh, for fuck's sake, it's next Monday. That's your fault! I don't even *like* him ...'

I end up standing on stage knowing I have been the cause of a domestic dispute which has not been alleviated by the need for most of the audience having to start their week by running round trying to get all the domestic duties done just so that they can spend two hours listening to someone else moan about domestic life. This irony is not lost on me or the audience. It means that the essential ingredient that makes observational comedy work, where you say something about the tensions that you find in domestic relationships that the audience recognise within themselves and laugh in recognition, is instead greeted with blank stares that say, 'Tell me something I *don't* know.'

I am not the only advocate of a daytime nap to enhance performance. Winston Churchill was another famous believer. He is said to have built it into his daily routine even during the tense times of World War II. He wasn't taking just a little doze in an armchair with his brandy in one hand and his cigar burning down to the fingers of his other. No, Winston was a professional sleeper. He would undress to his underwear and climb into bed, where he would then lie still and take twenty deep breaths. If he had not nodded off by then, he would conclude he had too much to do that day to sleep, whether it be defeating Nazi Germany and saving the world from unimaginable tyranny, or sending British troops to crush the striking miners in Tonypandy, thereby giving tacit state endorsement to the horrendous working conditions of those miners. Whatever it was, something was putting him off his sleep, so he got up.

Thankfully, I don't tend to have such considerations when I have my afternoon nap on tour. There is way less historic significance in what happens in my day, so I tend to nod off well before I have reached double figures in deep breaths. The only problem for me is that I do not live permanently on tour. I eventually have to come home after weeks or even months and have a period of re-acclimatising to normal life. During this period, my wife, Melanie, regularly finds me curled up in different corners of the house, like a cat, having a sleep while more important things are happening, such as the rest of the family sitting waiting for me so they can start dinner.

Afternoon sleeps definitely get more valuable as you grow older, not least because, as a short interlude in your day, they do not require the same 'post-sleep warm-up' you have in the morning. As I said, when I wake up I am filled with joy, surprise and apprehension, and the surprise is mainly that *I am still here*. It's not that I have the fear of death in my head when I go to bed – it's more that, for years, I have gone to bed thinking I will wake up in another life.

I never expected to be a comedian and never expected to have this life where someone would pay me to write a book. I never expected to have three sons who, by the time I am in my fifties and just working out who I am and what it means to be a man, are young men themselves. I never expected to still be married to the girl I met in the library when I was twenty-two years of age and full of hormones and dreams.

I never thought I would be The Me I Am Today. I often wake up surprised because, in a parallel universe, I know I am waking up as The Other Me. Because I can decide what The Other Me is like, I generally make sure that The Me I Am is better than The Me I Could Have Been. This morning, The Me I Am woke up in a gorgeous house with one of our dogs asleep at the foot of the bed while my beautiful wife lay fast sleep as sunlight was trying its best to seep through the last vestiges of the night's darkness, like a kitchen light through a net curtain. I walked downstairs, went to my study, opened my laptop, put the radio on Classic FM and sat writing this book.

The Other Me of my alternative life woke up in his dingy bedsit with a car alarm going off in the street outside and dogs barking. He could still taste the beer from last night's empty cans festooned around the room as he sat up and rubbed his hand over his bald head (I have decided that The Other Me does not have my genes and so has gone bald: not a stylish Pep Guardiola bald, more like a Bobby Charlton combover bald). He lowered his varicose-veined legs to the floor and, with a painful effort, rolled his twenty-stone frame off the bed to go to the bathroom for his morning piss. This always results in some slight dribble on his boxer shorts because he cannot actually see his own penis beneath his massive hairy belly. His phone was full of text messages from the various baby-mamas that he owed child support to, and his boss at the second-hand car dealership telling him he is likely to miss his monthly target again, so he is going to have to let him go. The Other Me glanced at his watch, sighed, farted and went back to bed.

That is the way I see The Other Me today, because I have made a conscious decision to make it a good day. There are other days when my wife won't talk to me, the kids think I'm a knob, my jeans feel too tight and I glance at myself in the mirror sideways on to see that I have changed shape and it looks as if I was once a foot taller and then a house fell on me and made everything about me more dense. I am thicker in just about every part of my body and what has not been squashed down is rolled up into a ball and fastened to the front of my belly.

Catching a glance at the decay of a once semi-athletic body is a unique form of sadness. I am used to being looked at on TV or on stage and so I have subconsciously learned to position myself front and centre of vision all the time, never sideways on. This means people see the mass of my body and the outline of my shape but can't see my hidden contours. A suit jacket can help maintain the myth that I am still in shape, and as I am fortunate enough to have broad shoulders there is a lot of cloth covering my midriff.

When I am alone, however, there is no escape. When it is just me in my underpants, trying to pull on a pair of jeans, and in the mirror I see the soufflé of fat that fills the space between the top of my underpants and my ribcage … well, those days I *know* that The Other Me is stood holding a gun to Robert De Niro's head, finger on the trigger while he looks straight into my eyes. I lower the gun, 'You know I wouldn't do it … not now I know you are my father.' There is a gasp in the audience, a knowing look from Robert De Niro with his head bowed and his mouth is in his classic half smile. We hear a gun shot, the screen goes black, the title music plays and the curtain closes. The Other Me is led on stage with Robert De Niro and Al Pacino to take questions as the standing ovation is ringing out. 'John, may I ask you,' begins a journalist, 'do you feel objectified because you perform the majority of this film naked from the waist up? Is that simply the studio using you as a sex object to sell the movie?'

Before The Other Me can speak, Robert De Niro and Al Pacino both respond with 'no's'. 'He is much more than a perfect torso,' says Al, to some amusement. 'Let me tell you something,' says Bob, 'I have waited years to work with this guy. When I heard he wanted me to play his father I was overjoyed. When I found out the lead character was a lifeguard and so would have his shirt off for most of the movie, I knew this guy could do it. But more than that … I have played many father-and-son scenes in my life,' he swallows hard, 'but this guy … this guy got me.' With tears in his eyes now. 'If I could have a son that was half the man this guy is, I gotta tell you …' Tears prevent him finishing his sentence, and as The Other Me moves to hug him to the applause and cheers at those gathered at the Cannes Film Festival Premier, he says in my ear 'Don't forget me at the Oscars!'

I feel apprehension when I wake up because I know I have to get up and I know something will hurt before I manage to get to the bathroom. With me, it's usually my feet. I have no explanation for this, but my feet, and in particular my heels, always hurt for the first few steps in the morning. Perhaps it's the fact that I am standing upright, which allows all of the hopes for the day to drain to their lowest natural point. By the time I have reached the bathroom, they have loosened up sufficiently to send the pain to my left knee on cold days, and to the space between my shoulder blades on every other. Pain in some part of your body is just something you get used to as you get older and your body breaks down. Knee and hip replacements become like love bites in your early teenage years; they are something you think you should be getting because everyone you know has them.

It used to be a different story. There was one particular part of my body that would wake up every morning before I did. Now, when I go for my morning pee, I sometimes feel I am waking up a sleeping mouse. It's not that all functional use has gone, despite the fact that testosterone falls in men in middle age and erectile dysfunction is nowadays so prevalent that foreplay has been replaced by taking a little blue pill.

This is all down to testosterone levels, which are highest during the madness of adolescence. As men get older their testosterone levels drop by about 1 per cent per year after the age of thirty. Women's hormonal levels decline after the menopause, which usually begins somewhere between forty-five and fifty-five. So men decline earlier and for longer – in fact, given that the male peak is around thirty and most of us may make ninety, we spend two-thirds of our life in decline. Accepting that most boys are useless till they are around twenty that means most men only have ten good years. Most dogs have more than that.

Happily, without being too boastful (I'm definitely not going to say, 'Touch wood!'), I have managed to swerve erectile dysfunction so far. My cock seems to have the work ethic of a touring comedian and thus does very little until required to perform. However, it has also developed its own form of jet-lag. Since I turned fifty, it seemed to have developed its own circadian rhythm and its 'morning glory' actually comes whenever it feels like it.

This would be wonderful if I knew when it was on the horizon, but I can be about to stand up in a café, or by the graveside at a funeral, and discover that the tightness in my trousers is no longer confined to my waist. I must admit that this has at various times led to feelings of both anxiety and pride. I have no doubt that when I am eventually in a nursing home, being wheeled around the garden not really knowing who I am, I will be the one the nurses will avoid like the plague. Because I will bore them with assertions that I used to be funny, while at the same time asking for a bed bath.

One thing that is certain about waking up is that every day you do it you are a little older than you ever have been before. But considering the alternative option of not waking up, I will always be grateful for the day ahead.

2.

HOW TO DRESS

WHEN I WAS FORTY, I did some stand-up about my son taking my new training shoes and wearing them. The stand-up basically went like this:

When a man reaches forty, you know you have reached the stage in your life where wearing brand new white training shoes is a gamble. Any man in his forties wearing brand new white training shoes is taking a chance because, instead of looking cool, there is a very good likelihood that by wearing brand new white training shoes you will look like someone else dressed you, and that you should be holding hands with another responsible adult. I recently bought a brand new pair of white Adidas that I thought were a new style but the assistant told me was a retro look. I still took them to be a new style because they had been in fashion and out and back in again without me noticing.

A few days later I was getting the lads together to go out for a pizza when my fifteen-year-old son walked down the stairs wearing my new training shoes. My brand new white training shoes. That's how big he is: size nine.

I told him: 'Son, take them off, they are my brand new shoes.' He just looked at me and said, 'No-oo!'

His voice was breaking, which made him sound like Scooby Doo. It also made it hard to argue with him, because it's difficult to be angry and laugh at the same time.

I said, 'Listen, I am not asking you, I am telling you! Get up those stairs and take them off.' To which he just looked at me and said, 'No. I won't.'

That is the moment that every father of a son knows will come one day but it still hits you like a train. It's the moment the little lion takes on the big lion, like in a David Attenborough documentary. I knew that if I backed down, he would be the big lion and I would be the old lion who has to watch the other lions eat the zebra. I would be in our garden on Christmas Day looking through the kitchen window while he would be sat in my seat.

So, I said, 'Son. Do what I say and take those trainers off now!' And he just looked in my eyes and said, 'Make me!'

For the first time in the fifteen years of his life I could see in his eyes he was thinking: 'I can take you!' And, for my first time in the fifteen years of his life, I was thinking, 'There's a chance he could take me!'

There is nothing more humbling than thinking you are about to get your head kicked in ... with your own shoes.

That piece of material was true. The incident actually happened and I did think buying white training shoes were a gamble because I found not knowing what to wear harder at forty than I did at fifty. This was is in large part because my life was changing so rapidly at forty. I was going through a sort of mid-life crisis and it changed how I wore clothes. I didn't start wearing tight jeans and pointy shoes to attract a twenty-five-year-old secretary and run off with her in my open-top sports car. My sort-of mid-life crisis was less predictable than that – although it was possibly a bigger gamble.

A month before my fortieth birthday, I cut all ties with my previous life to become a full-time comedian. My previous job had been as the sales and marketing manager of a specialised division within a pharmaceutical company. I say specialised because I was responsible for a team selling a product called Tacrolimus (Prograf), which is part of the immunosuppression family of drugs, and was licensed for use in organ transplantation to stop patients from rejecting their organs.

At this stage, I had been doing stand-up in my spare time for nearly five years. This involved working in the day and then driving in my company car to the venues, changing out of my business suit and going on stage in jeans and a shirt. To me, it had felt too much of a clash of worlds to walk on stage in the Marks & Spencer suit I had been wearing all day. In my head, suits were for work and jeans and the like were for on stage – what you wear when you are not working and you're enjoying yourself.

As I turned forty, I went into a new reality where my after-work wardrobe became the one I wore all day. I could now wear jeans all the time, but I soon began to feel that I wasn't ready for 'work' if I wasn't getting changed before I went on stage. I had a wardrobe of suits that I had worn in my old life but it was apparent to me that turning up at a comedy club dressed like a sales and marketing manager was not exactly the showbiz image I was striving for.

Then I saw it. It was in a dress agency shop in London. Dress agencies are basically posh second-hand shops that only stock high-end clothes that are no longer wanted by their previous owners, but which are too good to be lost in the piles of tatty old clothes in a normal charity shop. The dress agency will either buy the clothes from the owner outright, or sell them on their behalf and give them a cut. It's far less benevolent than donating your clothes to a charity shop but they *do* provide an answer to the question of, 'What shall I do with this? It's just too expensive to give away for the benefit of others!' The answer is to sell it to someone who appreciates its expense, and who will be the conduit between you and the charity shop by wearing the clothes in front of everyone they know, so they can present themselves as someone who would buy such a thing new. Once everyone they know has seen the item, it can be passed further down the second-hand line.

I saw the suit in the window of a dress agency and it was love at first sight. It was a purple suit with a turquoise lining that I would never have been brave enough to wear in my previous professional life. To be fair, I suspect that talking to a Professor of Transplant Surgery about their immunosuppression regime while dressed like a sax player from a 1980s ska band would have been frowned upon. But to be dressed like that standing under stage lights in a comedy club ... that is what I was born to do, and it is what that suit was made for.

I immediately went in and asked to try it on. One good thing is that I am not in any way averse to wearing second-hand clothes. I did plenty of that for most of my life as a kid. I was the youngest of four, with my brother Eddie being five years older than me and my sisters Carol and Kathy being in-between us. So, for a large part of my life, hand-me-downs formed most of my wardrobe (not always an easy process when inheriting clothes from two older sisters).

That was in the 1970s and the 1980s, when clothes were a major investment for the family and would be worn to the extent that, by the time they were thrown out, they were totally worn out.

Today, cheap clothing is the norm and people have many more clothes than they need. But with less than 1 per cent of the world's clothing being manufactured with any consideration of environmental sustainability, I guess there is a duty for us all to try and extend the life of the clothing that passes through our hands.

None of those things, I must confess, were going through my mind when I saw the purple suit. I just thought I would look cool in it, so I went in and tried it on. The label said that it was made by Ozwald Boateng and, well, that said it all. Ozwald Boateng is a tall, slim, handsome black man: a renowned fashion designer who has won many awards for his designs, which tend to be sharp-cut suits with bold and creative colours. Basically, he makes clothes that look great on tall, slim, handsome, black men. I was a slightly squat middle-aged white man and yet, despite suspecting the suit was not owned by anyone who looked remotely like me, I could not wait to put it on.

I had no problem with the jacket. It fitted like a glove. The trousers were more of a challenge and had clearly previously been owned by someone taller and thinner than me. However, the shop offered to arrange the alterations. This is another brilliant thing about a dress agency as opposed to a normal charity shop. I can't imagine Oxfam being able to cope if people started asking for extensive alterations on a pair of trousers that they were buying for £1.50. However, in a dress agency, where you are paying a decent price (the suit was £145, with £12 for alterations), it's all part of the service.

I don't know if the suit's previous owner was a tall, slim, handsome black man, but as soon as I saw myself in it, that is what I felt like: smooth, cool and invincible. It was the perfect suit to wear 'going to work' in my new life on stage. It said everything I needed it to say. In every dressing room where I wore it and looked in the mirror, the suit spoke to me, in the voice of Barry White, saying, *'Uh-huh, Johnny, you look cool. You look like you belong, baby. You look like you're going to make the audience . . . aaah . . . laugh. You got this and don't forget, sugar, if you wear a purple suit and you ain't funny . . . there's nowhere to go, baby. So, don't be shit.'*

I loved that suit and it is one of the last items of clothing that I did virtually wear out. In fact, in my early years as a professional comedian, I knew I could never afford another Ozwald Boateng suit so I made the mistake of trying to get an imitation.

Hong Kong Foolery

I had been booked to do a weekend of gigs in Hong Kong with two other comedians. There was a UK-based Canadian, Sean Collins, with a very sharp, laid-back way of telling stories that I never tire of listening to, and Steve Royle. Steve is a physical comedian from Lancashire who was the court jester at Camelot Theme Park before becoming a circuit comedian. I have never seen anyone as good at telling jokes while juggling.

The weekend shows in Hong Kong are part of the odd world of gigs you sometimes get offered on the circuit. They were booked by a UK promoter whom I immediately didn't like as he flew in business class while telling us we had done well to be upgraded to premium economy. I'm also pretty sure he made a lot more from the gigs than we did.

We did three gigs in Hong Kong in an Indian restaurant to expats who wanted a reminder of what they were missing by having a curry and listening to some English jokes. They lacked many of the reference points of recent British life because they weren't in the UK, so once the joy of hearing an accent from the homeland had waned, they were a good but rather passive audience.

These gigs paid £250 each. You flew out on Wednesday and back on Sunday night to arrive in the UK on Monday. This meant you earned about £300 more than you would on a normal weekend in comedy clubs at home and as you were fed, and the flights and hotel were paid for, it was basically a free, well-paid weekend away.

The other big plus point of the trip – and many of the comedians who had been before us had done this – was that you could take advantage of being in Hong Kong by getting a suit or two made by the super-quick tailors there. It was the only real chance for a circuit comedian to get a genuine made-to-measure suit and, as my purple Ozwald Boateng number was on its last legs, I was looking for a replacement.

We had the name of a tailor and so Steve and I set out to find him. Sean was too cool for a suit in those days, preferring to do his act in a black three-quarter length leather jacket. Now, you can get away with that with a North American accent, but I knew it would not work for me as I would both look and sound like Jimmy Corkhill.* The taxi driver dropped Steve and me outside a

---

* *If you get that reference from* Brookside, *well done, and you are welcome. If you do not know what I am talking about, I apologise, but no explanation will be given. Sometimes in life you either know or you don't know, and this reference to Jimmy Corkhill will either make you laugh or bemuse you. That's just the way it is.*

small shop. It didn't appear to be an establishment that was likely to be an outfitter to the comedians of Great Britain. Nevertheless, we went straight in and, sure enough, we were in the right place. It was like a Bond film where Daniel Craig arrives in Hong Kong in disguise as a Chinese peasant farmer. Once he knows he is clear of anyone following him, he walks into a nondescript door to find a world of activity inside. They would already know his suit size, and he would walk out minutes later, looking charismatic, without a hint that he had ever even seen a paddy field.

The shop we walked in was almost like that. *Almost.* Before we had even said a word, the proprietor knew why we were there. He knew we were English comedians who – like those who had come before us – were doing gigs in an Indian restaurant to a barely interested audience, but who had aspirations that one day a made-to-measure suit would benefit our developing careers – provided, that was, that a tailor could do it for £200, in three days, from one set of measurements.

In fact, the tailor didn't even have to measure me, I just gave him my purple Ozwald Boateng suit and asked him to copy it in a different colour. I settled for red with yellow lining. Steve went for light blue but he also showed the added commitment of getting measured properly rather than lazily handing something else over and asking for it to be reproduced. Steve's attention to detail was to prove time well spent. The suits were delivered to the hotel as we checked out and I took my first ever made-to-measure suit home with pride. I had visions of being known as The Comedian in the Sharp Suits. After all, I had a purple suit that was being hammered yet still looked great under the lights, and now I had a red one to add to the collection. It wasn't until I got home that I discovered that my new made-to-measure suit had clearly been made-to-measure for somebody else. There was no way it was even close to being like the Ozwald Boateng suit it was meant to mimic. The sleeves were not even the same length. One barely showed my fingers and the other was halfway up my forearm.

I am not entirely blaming the tailors because I know plenty of comedians that they made great suits for. I even saw Steve a year later, doing his act with his light blue suit on, and it looked great. I looked at his arms closely, because one thing I am pretty sure of is that when you are juggling, having arms the same length is fairly essential. As for me, I only wore that red suit once. I used the long arm to hold the microphone to see if I could get away with it and try to disguise the sleeve length, but it just didn't work. Wearing a red suit with the sleeve of the other arm halfway up my forearm made me look like a Duran Duran tribute act paying homage to the 'Rio' video.

The episode did teach me a good lesson for my stand-up career. Stage clothes should not distract an audience. As soon as an audience is thinking 'Why is he wearing *that*?' you have started to lose them. At the time, I could ill-afford to write off the £200 but the suit was beyond hope and so off it headed to Oxfam. I just hope that a colour-blind person with one arm longer than the other found it and made the most of it.

I had to wait patiently until my career had moved on sufficiently to get a made-to-measure Ozwald Boateng suit. It was for my first BBC Saturday night series, *John Bishop's Britain*, in 2010. The production company had a clothing budget and I made it clear that I craved an Ozwald Boateng made-to-measure suit. It had to be a quick turnaround as production was about to start so they told me it would cost a premium but they would push it through.

I was measured a couple of times, had the suit delivered and wore it for the shows.

I was told afterwards that the suit cost £6,250. It was the most expensive piece of clothing I have ever owned, or intend to ever own. Had I known it was so much I would have said no, but I didn't and so the suit was delivered. It was an absolute disaster. It looked terrible. I have no idea why my purple suit, which I assumed was originally made for a tall, slim, handsome black man, looked fantastic on me, while the one made-to-measure for me, bespoke for a squat middle-aged white man, was so awful, but it was. I only wore it for the first half of the series and then gave up.

How could this be? Perhaps longing to fill the purple suit had made me hold myself differently? Perhaps in the intervening years I had changed shape so much that it was like putting a tie on a giraffe – there was just too much to cover? I don't know, but that suit hardly got worn, and pound-for-pound it is probably the most expensive thing I have ever owned, including a house, unless I ever buy a house where I have to pay £2,000 every time I walk in the door. And the production company had stumped up for it! I have never been so bold as to request anything like that since and I never will.

To be fair to Ozwald Boateng, he has invited me in to have another suit made as a replacement and said he will personally oversee the manufacture to ensure it is as good as it can be. However, I haven't yet managed to find the time … or, should I say, I haven't yet managed to get the body shape that I am happy for a tall, handsome, black man to measure. There is a special kind of disappointment to have someone whom you want to look like measuring you. It's like Robbie Williams standing in front of you while you sing 'Angels' at him. No matter what you both say to be nice, both of you will be disappointed.* So, I will carry on looking in the dress agencies for another cast-off.

XL Is the New XXXL

The changing life expectations of the middle-aged in the twenty-first century have created a whole new industry: fashion for those whose looks and bodies require clothing to flatter and hide, rather than enhance and reveal. When I was growing up, my mum and dad seemed to decide what clothes they liked when they were thirty and stuck with them. Now, it's acceptable to try and keep up with trends you see in magazines, even though there is nobody in those magazines who looks remotely like you. The fashion industry in the UK is said to be worth £32 billion, and older people account for an ever-growing percentage of that. Even over-sixty-fives spend £6.7bn a year on clothes in Britain. Clothing the grey-tops is big business.

It's not just the market that is growing: the size of the clothes is, too. You can now buy men's clothing in XXXL sizes in standard high-street shops. Just think about that. Enough people buy these sizes for retailers to think that it is worth holding them in stock for the next wave of massive people that come in through the double doors and up the (very slow) escalator. In the past, to be that size gave you a chance of getting on the regional television news

---

* *I know – I have done it.*

and becoming a local tourist attraction. Not any longer. The level of obesity in the UK has reached epidemic proportions, with the middle-aged definitely more than playing their part.

The average waist size of men in the UK is thirty-eight inches and the average dress size for women is sixteen. Obviously, some people have medical issues that affect them, and I don't want to get into fat-shaming, but on a national level we can only assume nowadays that the people singing 'Who eat all the pies?' are asking a rhetorical question – because statistics suggest that we *all* did.

Clothing brands have not failed to notice this trend. They have taken the very canny move of encouraging more shoppers to buy their brands by flattering them that they are not as big as they actually are. As average clothes sizes have gone up, people prefer to lie to themselves that they can't be fat if their clothing label says they're not. So Small has become XS, Medium has turned into Small and Large has become Medium. Extra-Large (XL) is Large, XXL is now XL, XXXL is XXL, Massive is now XXXL, and Size-That-Is-Worthy-Of-A-Channel-4-Documentary has now got its own page on the Jacamo site.

The challenge of when to wear age-appropriate clothing is a difficult one because we keep changing what is age-appropriate. There are many men who are still in the clothes that they wore when they were twenty-five when they looked like the Modfather himself, Paul Weller, with a feather-cut hair style, tight trousers and Fred Perry T-shirt. Twenty-five years later, when not even Paul Weller dresses like that, they look too old for the clothes that they are wearing. Their faces are too wrinkled and their clothes don't hang right. Like Yoda at a Jam concert they do look.

Often, these men make the terrible mistake of combining the clothes of their youth with a desire to maintain the hair colour of their youth. I have never understood men who dye their hair. Very few of them look good. Those who commit to dying their hair also need to consider how their face looks and attempt to keep that young, or at least make an effort. A baggy, wrinkled face hanging down below freshly dyed black hair just looks wrong. If you are not careful, you are in danger of making your face look like a scrotum with a big nose, and that's not a look anyone can really carry off.

In middle age, women do at least seem to have more advice and a whole industry dedicated to helping them with their clothing choices. They have magazines, online articles, fashion tipsters and friends who will go with them, help to choose clothes, cajole them into trying new things, give honest feedback and do all they can to help each them look good. Men have some of those things – there are style magazines that helpfully tell us where we can spend a few hundred quid on a pair of socks – but what we lack, particularly in middle age, is the support of the people who know us best – friends.

This is because most men don't notice what any of their mates are wearing. It would be a generalisation to say that gay men dress better than straight men at any age, but I would suggest it is certainly true in middle age. Were it not for wives and children buying things for birthdays and Christmas, most middle-aged men would walk around naked, or in something they bought with their first wages thirty years ago.

We simply don't have the interest in fashion that I think we should. I have never seen a group of middle-aged men walking around the shops together, looking to help get their mate Kevin a new shirt. None of my mates have ever picked something off the rack and brought it over to me, saying 'You *have* to try this – it will work great with the jeans you've got, and you can wear it to the darts match next week!'

But times are changing. The days when middle-aged men simply bought trousers with elasticated waistbands and cardigans have gone. Cardigans, for a start, are now called knitwear, which is the fashion equivalent of putting up a white flag. Once you realise that your best look is knitwear, you have effectively given up on fashion. In wearing something where it is impossible to see where you end and the clothing begins, you are accepting that you have no shape of your own: you simply have a body mass that needs covering.

The Waft of Shame

When the first hints of summer arrive, so does the moment of truth and disappointment that can best be summed up by ... *the waft of shame*.

I first experienced the waft of shame about two years ago. I had been on tour in the winter and had an injury in my left knee which prevented me doing my normal exercise. When you are over fifty you can't get a note from your mum to excuse you from exercise, so I have always found a 'knee problem' is generally the best excuse. When you say, 'I have a knee problem', nobody is surprised. You are in your fifties: it's expected.

When my tour finished, I had a knee operation, and so began the spring on crutches with nothing to do except relax and recuperate. As soon as the first sunny day arrived, I couldn't wait to put on shorts and a T-shirt and sit in the garden. The shorts fitted fine. Like all of my trousers and jeans, the shorts decided where my waist should be and stopped there. This means my waist is now on a slant: slightly higher on the back and lower at the front where the shorts provide a platform for my tummy to rest on.

I put the T-shirt on. My head went through its hole fine. My arms did the same, and I pulled the T-shirt down. The shoulders sat where they should, and then I rolled the T-shirt over my torso. Looking down, it seemed OK. I couldn't see the bottom of the T-shirt so I assumed it was where it should be. It was then that I felt the waft of shame – a light frontal breeze between the base of the shirt and the waist of the shorts.

The two items of clothing sat comfortably together at the back but at the front it looked like they had had an argument. My T-shirt seemed to be pulling itself away from my shorts and using my belly to climb up. I have had many disappointments in my life, but few matched the moment I looked in the mirror and saw that my favourite T-shirt from the summer before now looked like I had stolen it from a child. The three-inch gap between the bottom of the shirt and the top of my shorts allowed a draught to circulate and gently stroke the hairs on my belly in a way that would have seemed relaxing were it not so tragic. I had become *that man*: the one who wears clothes that do not fit because he is deluded enough to think the world will not notice.

Here's the thing: the world *does* notice. *I* notice when I see the classic middle-aged man look, standing with a pint in one hand, slightly leaning back for balance, a gap between his trousers and T-shirt that allows the world a glimpse at his flabby tummy. The sad thing is many men don't see this in themselves, and that is partly because it literally feels like it comes overnight. You wake up one day fatter than you were when you went to bed, and then that trend continues forever.

It doesn't help that we are bombarded with images of men like Tom Cruise, Bradley Cooper and even Hugh Jackman. These are men who are past forty but who somehow got there without picking up any belly on the way. Woman have been pressured with images of how they should look for decades, but this is a new thing for men and we don't really know how to handle it. In fact, judging from what I see on a day-to-day basis, we do our best to ignore it completely. Given the effort it takes to look like Bradley Cooper does on magazine covers, it is easier just to carry on eating buns and buying XXXL clothes.

The biggest paradox of all is the number of overweight people in sportswear. By its very name, sportswear should be something you wear to play sport. Yet walk around any shopping centre in the UK and you will find this is not the case. Go into Greggs and you will see more tracksuits than you will in the local gym, even though the only muscles being exercised in there are the many jaws chomping down on doughnuts.

I totally understand people wearing sportswear for comfort. As I write this, I am sat in shorts and a Nike tracksuit top. This is partly because it's comfortable, and partly because I always go through this ritual of putting on gym kit just in case I might go to the gym. For anyone who has ever suffered from anything like writer's block, the best way to resolve it is to put your gym kit on. It's surprising how motivated to write you get when the alternative is going to the gym.

Wearing gym clothes is fine if you look like you might actually know where the gym is. But wearing gym clothes when you are the size of a small bungalow is disingenuous. Your clothes are making a promise that your body simply cannot keep. This is even worse when it comes to replica football shirts. I assume that all of those replica shirts are made in the same factory as the actual team kit, probably in China. What on earth goes through the minds of the people who have to pack a XXXL shirt with a number eleven on the back? Some of them must be thinking, 'That Mo Salah hasn't half let himself go!"

Death to Smart Casual

The very worst option when it comes to men's fashion is 'smart casual'. Just *what* is that supposed to mean? You can't be both: it's like being a small-tall man, or fat-thin, or fast-slow. They are opposites, and when they are not opposites then it's just confusing. Men see clothes as a binary choice. Smart is suits, trousers, neat jumper, jacket, shirt and shoes. Casual is jeans, T-shirts, trainers and a sweatshirt. The bit in the middle is just too confusing.

I was still working in the real world when Dress-down Friday was born. The idea was that people in offices could 'dress down'

---

* *It is worth noting here that I am directing my comments towards those of us who suffer what is known as middle-aged spread. There is humour in the shared experience of your body giving up on any pretension to be fit agile or desirable. This not a chapter looking to poke fun or body shame those people of size who would wish themselves to be different but through genes or lifestyle and emotional issues struggle to achieve this. I accept that in later chapters I poke fun at American people of size because the situation simply would not have been notable had size not played a part but I hope what I am saying here is taken in context and is not perceived to be condoning or engaging in bullying. On stage or in a live situation I would have the option to control the balance of how this is presented – you have less control over the written word so I felt it important to put it in context.*

for the day. It's a bit like 'Own-clothes Day' at school, except that you don't have to put a pound in company funds and the boss doesn't let you play board games for the last hour of the day. The idea was basically: *Hey, let's all relax and see ourselves as real people and not corporate squares!*

The downside of this innovation was that, for a man, a suit hides a multitude of sins, including his lack of fashion sense. Unless you put it on backwards it's hard to get a suit wrong. When Dress-down Friday began, however, we all got a glimpse into the world of work colleagues that changed how we saw them forever.

I had one boss who seemed to think that Dress-down Friday really meant Golf Clothes Day, as that was all he ever wore on these days. At first I assumed that he must be playing golf on the way into work or on the way home. But when he continued coming into the office dressed like Seve Ballesteros in the winter, when it was still dark when we got into work and dark when we left, I realised that that wasn't the case. Now, as we all know, golf clothing has a fairly wide spectrum. You can look sporty and athletic like Tiger Woods, or you can look like Huggy Bear from *Starsky & Hutch*. My boss tended to lean more towards the latter, and soon it became increasingly difficult to take him seriously, dressed as he was halfway between a clown and a pimp.

Once we had to have a disciplinary meeting with one of our sales reps, and my boss walked in wearing yellow trousers and a pastel blue T-shirt, with a red pullover hanging across his shoulders like a shawl. We sat the sales rep down to review his previous appraisal and how he wasn't performing against the objectives that he had been set. It wasn't easy for me to tell him with a serious face that he was not meeting the company's expectations when my boss was sat there looking like a fruit pastel. His yellow trousers had no place being worn by anyone who was not a Motown backing singer and, while the polo shirt was almost acceptable, the red jumper most certainly wasn't.

The main problem wasn't the colour – although the clash of primary colours of the yellow and red was an eyesore – but the way he wore it. Sometimes a middle-aged man has to carry a jumper that he is not sure he is going to wear. As you get older, you are not as sure as you were in your youth how hot your body is going to be as the day goes on. You are no longer sure that a T-shirt will do the job because your wealth of life experience has taught you that it might get a bit chilly during the day, and then you will wish you had a pullover. So you face the dilemma of having it with you but not actually wearing it.

You could carry a bag, except that you clearly won't because you are a man, and you know that if you decide to wear the jumper you will end up having the new problem of carrying an empty bag around. Not only is this something that never looks cool, but an empty bag also suggests that you have forgotten something, or that you have been kicked out of home without enough time to pack. But in the absence of a bag, you then have to decide how to carry the pullover. You could simply carry it, but that would mean that one of your hands is then permanently full. There is every chance that you will put it down somewhere, because carrying something all day is annoying for anyone, and once you put it down there is at least a fifty–fifty chance you are going to lose it.

Men have an incredible ability to lose things. In any house, it is always the man looking for his keys, his wallet, his phone, his ambition, his sex drive, his energy and his sense of meaning (well, definitely the first few, anyway). My theory is that it's in our DNA as part of the evolutionary process. In most ancient societies, men were the hunters and so it is within our nature to need to hunt. That's why we lose things: we need to be hunting something, and in the absence of hunting for food or being chased by a lion, hunting for your car keys while the wife and kids are waiting at the door gives us the same adrenaline rush.

Sadly, the chances of you losing the jumper increase the older you get. If you accept my theory, as an older member of a caveman tribe you would need to continually show yourself worthy of remaining in the group by proving you could still hunt. And the older you become, the more annoying it is to go shopping to replace anything. Your clothes become moulded to your shape, so going back to the same shop to buy the same thing in the same size does not always yield the same result. It feels too small, it doesn't suit you, and you end up not replacing the thing you lost as you realise you never actually looked good in it anyway.

To avoid having to go shopping for another jumper, men have decided that the best thing to do is to *wear* the jumper without actually *wearing* it. We tie the jumper somewhere on our bodies, using the sleeves to keep it in place. There are only two basic ways of doing this and they say everything about a man's social class and his age.*

The first option is to wear it around the waist, where the neck of the pullover is placed on the small of the back and the sleeves are brought round to the front and tied in a double knot. This is the

---

* *This is true unless you are a cricket umpire and can tie the jumpers of an entire cricket team to various parts of your body, becoming more wool than man, yet still being able to judge whether a ball travelling at 100mph grazed a bat 20 metres away.*

way to carry a jumper if you are young and/or working class and I would always go for it. It leaves your hands free, the pullover is immediately accessible, and ever since I was a kid, I have liked the idea that I might look like a Red Indian from behind.

The other option was the one chosen by my boss with his red pullover – in fact, with any pullover he wore on Dress-down Friday – and is the preserve of middle-class, middle-aged men. Here, the pullover is placed on the shoulders so that the arms hang in the front of the torso. Then you take one sleeve and gently overlap it with the other to hold the jumper in place. The waist method requires a serious knot, whereas the shoulders method needs greater subtlety: a tight knot would bring it to your neck and thus lose the casual effect desired.

When men employ the shoulder method, they seem to be saying to the world, *'Hey, that's right, I am ready for minor changes in the climate, and I have the clothing at hand should I require it, but let's be cool and not mention it, because I am just an ordinary guy like you, even though we both know that I am better than you at just about everything.'*

When I see someone wearing their jumper like a shawl, I just immediately think, 'Cock.'

I am not for one minute trying to justify my prejudice – it's stupid to judge a man purely on the way he carries a jumper – but I can't help it. There is just something about seeing a pullover on a man's shoulders that says something about them as a person. Oddly, I find it much less offensive if the person wearing his pullover that way happens to be European: for some reason that's what I would expect of them, because I have always thought that European men were simply better at wearing clothes. They have tanned skin and waist lines that suggest they can enjoy a glass of wine with dinner without thinking that if the bottle has been opened, it may as well be finished.

This was brought home to me in my days in my sales job when I used to have to go to international business meetings. I soon discovered that my European male counterparts always looked fabulous. They didn't wear anything overstated, just well-cut suits, trouser–jacket combinations that matched perfectly, and shoes that looked like they had never been worn in the rain. At every meeting, I always felt their crisp, sharp clothes resonated class, while my clothes seemed to hold self-doubt and low self-esteem in their very fabric. The difference was so pronounced that I began to think they were receiving a bonus clothing allowance.

I actually asked one Italian colleague how he always looked so smart and he gave me a really interesting answer. He said that because the weather is so warm in Italy, people sweat more and so wear out their clothes more quickly. This means they buy new clothes far more often than we do. What he was *really* saying was, *'Go and buy some new clothes, you scruffy bastard!'* but he was far too diplomatic for that.

Vest Intentions

As you get older, the question of what you wear every day to face the world gets easier in some ways – you can always just give up and retreat into pullovers and slacks, though I'm not ready to do that yet – and harder in others. Some of life's eternal questions get more pressing as you hit middle age, and one of them is that eternal quandary – is it ever OK to wear a vest?

For me, it's a straight no. I have never seen a middle-aged man wear a vest as an outer garment and look good. If you wear a vest like that, it is like wearing your underpants on the outside of your trousers. They are just not meant to be there. For a man in his fifties, going about your business in a vest is akin to a statement. It's putting yourself somewhere between a wife beater and a social outcast. You're telling the world that either you live on your own, or you don't live with anybody who's prepared to tell you just how bad you look.

Wearing a vest with no shirt might be OK when you are twenty and you are in a nightclub in Ibiza but it's not when you are a middle-aged man. For one thing, your body is working against you. When you are a middle-aged man you have hairs growing out of your body that you don't even know about. Unless you are very unlucky, you don't tend to have hairy shoulders in your twenties. It's a very different story in your fifties. Once you see hairy shoulders, you know all you need to know about their owner. *Nobody* has hairy shoulders and grooms their other areas of body hair – the shoulders are a window into the pubic foliage that you know will cover the rest of their body. They are basically Chewbacca in a vest.

I have a gay friend who has told me that such hirsute men are regarded in some quarters as attractive. In fact, they are seen as an ever better catch when they are big fellows, and are known as bears. Some gay clubs have specific bear nights where I would imagine it's almost obligatory to wear a vest. You are definitely getting what it says on the tin when you wake up next to a fat, hairy bloke after a bear night. My friend is a slim, hairy man so I asked him if men of his type had a name. He said, 'otters'. I had no reply.

As you get to the age I am now, hairs grow everywhere. I look at our holiday photos and I have hairs that amaze me. I even have hairs in the small of my back – Melanie noticed them the other day. I have absolutely no idea where they have come from: it's like somebody must have just come along in the night and stuck them there. What can you do about them? No barber that I know offers a shave-the-lower-back-service.

And I do know some amazing barbers. I went to a Turkish barber just the other week. He did the wet shave, which is great, and then he did this thing where he got cotton buds used for cleaning ears and asked me, 'Do you want the wax?' I had no idea what he was talking about, so I said, 'Yes, whatever.' He got the cotton buds, put them in a hot tub of wax and then shoved them right up my nose. I wasn't expecting *that*. I sat there for a few minutes with the earbuds hanging out of my nose and then, when they had gone hard, the barber yanked them both out, pulling all the hairs from the inside of my nose out as he did it. *Jesus, it was painful!* And so it should have been, bearing in mind that it had taken me fifty-two years to grow those nasal hairs. Some of them were longer than the hairs on my head.

That's the kind of service that Turkish barbers provide – but not even they will invite you to take your shirt off and lean over their chair so they can take care of the hair at the bottom of your back. Nobody is doing that. Maybe there's a gap in the market, because all men of my age will have those hairs on their back. Maybe we need to visit a sheep shearer.

I'm not trying to get all of the vest factories closed down here. I think it is fine as an undergarment, whatever age you are, as long as other people can't see it. Maybe it's a nationality thing. I remember as a kid seeing the Fonz in *Happy Days* in his skimpy T-shirt and he looked really cool. But a middle-aged British man in a vest will always evoke either *Steptoe & Son* or Stan Ogden.*

A similar garment that I don't get on with as I get older is the gilet. The gilet seems to be for people who have decided that their arms are in a different climate from the rest of their body. They think *as long as my torso is warm, my arms will automatically be warm too* – well, how exactly does that work? I reckon you should only wear a gilet if you are French and pissed off enough to speak while waving your arms to get them warm.

A Load of Pants

But it's not just deciding how to cover your torso that can be a nightmare for middle-aged men. Your bottom half can be a mine-field as well. And in moments of doubt and insecurity, who else would we turn to but fashion designers?

Tom Ford is one of the best male fashion designers in the world. I read an interview that he did not so long ago, where the journalist asked him a very good question: 'Not every man can afford to go out and buy a Tom Ford suit or an entire Tom Ford wardrobe – what is your advice to those people?' And Tom Ford said, 'Every man can afford to make sure that they buy fresh underwear every year. They have to clear out their underwear and make sure it's fresh. When you put on fresh underwear, you are starting the day by telling yourself, "I'm worth something."'

---

* *Much like Jimmy Corkhill, Stan Ogden is a British cultural reference point for middle-aged men that you either get or you don't. No explanation is needed or, indeed, permitted.*

A big part of me buys into what Tom is talking about. When I was a lot younger and just married, I was a semi-professional footballer playing in the Northern Premier League for teams like Southport, Hyde and Winsford. We would be getting changed before the matches, and I'd have a glance around the dressing-room at the other lads' undies. This was when Calvin Klein and the like were just coming in, and everyone else would be proudly wearing them. I would be there, thinking to myself: *You spend £25 on a pair of undies? You must be fucking mad!* Then I would look down at my own pants, and I'd be wearing a tattered old pair that had 'Birthday Boy' written on them.

Before Marky Mark started advertising it, male underwear wasn't a fashion and I think that was probably not a bad thing. When I was first married and we didn't have a lot of money, I distinctly remember thinking that the last thing I wanted to spend money on was something that nobody would ever see. Why would I waste money on pants? I was married so the element of surprise had gone and so why spend what cash we had on new underpants – it would be like wrapping a present up after it had been opened and then doing it again and again. Once you know what is inside the package (as it were), it becomes much less important to have it wrapped up.

I remember having a very bizarre underpants-related incident on a work trip to Spain. While I was still working for the pharmaceutical company, I went to a conference in Barcelona. I was going to be there for three days. Melanie and I had just had our first baby, everything in the house and in our lives was chaos, and I had packed and left in a rush. I got to Barcelona, unpacked my bag and found I hadn't packed any underpants.

This didn't seem like a big problem. I was staying by the Nou Camp stadium and just down the road was a department store called *El Corte Inglés*, which is like a Spanish take on Marks & Spencer. I wandered down to the store and up the escalator to the menswear department, where I found myself amidst a vast array of Catalonian underwear.

I managed to find an assistant who spoke English and told him, 'I'm after underpants.' He nodded, took me over to one side of the section and showed me a box with some pants in. 'These are perfect for you,' he told me. I lifted the pants out of the box and there was … *a weight to them.* I thought, hang on, pants don't usually weigh this much. I had never held underpants that weighed anything.

I looked at them more closely and they were padded in the rear. *Padded!* They were like an underpants version of a Wonderbra! I looked at the guy, and I thought, you cheeky bastard! He had obviously looked me up and down and thought, you need a lift. Your arse is saggy. I just couldn't believe that a) he thought I needed them, and b) that anybody bought them, ever.

The disappointment factor must be huge. It's like when you meet a girl in a Wonderbra and you get to take it off, and you realise, *Oh … there's nothing there.* So imagine the disappointment for a poor man or woman who thinks they have copped off with a really fit Spanish waiter, gets to the bedroom where he drops his kecks and his arse is hanging down past his big, baggy scrotum? It's not going to be a good moment, for either of them. I didn't buy the padded underpants.

Now I am in middle age, I have gone totally the other way from the days when I was frugal about my pants. Over the years, I have tried out various different kinds of underwear. I wore boxer shorts for a while, but I found it was just like wearing a pair of curtains. They were too loose and I didn't like them. I feel like I need someone, or something, to give my bollocks a cuddle, so I've settled on wearing clingy hipster pants. I've got way too many of them. It's bonkers. Joking aside, I probably have a pair of pants for every day of the month.*

I've got a bit of a thing with shoes, as well. When you're a kid – and this was particularly true for me, coming from a not well-off family – you have two pairs of shoes. You have your winter shoes and your summer pumps. The best shoes I ever had as a boy were black school shoes that had animal footprints moulded into the sole so that when you walked through mud it would look like there were tigers about. Our council estate was covered in tiger footprints like it was a safari park. The shoes also had a compass in the heel. This was the most useless place imaginable to put a compass in a pair of shoes, as there is absolutely no chance of seeing the compass when you have your shoes on, but it gave you a sense of adventure that you were not just wearing a pair of shoes, you had part of a survival kit on. I suppose, for a manufacturer to go down a similar route today, they would have to put a satnav in the heel.

I also remember having a pair of orange pumps with black stars on. I have never worn any garment since that I loved more. I happened across an old photograph of me wearing them recently and somehow all of the happy memories of my childhood felt encapsulated in that pair of tatty orange pumps. That is what shoes can mean to you, particularly when you do not have dozens of pairs and getting a new pair is always such a big deal.

---

* *The weird thing is, when my lads come to stay with us it turns into a fight as to who gets the pants. I don't know whose pants I am wearing half the time. I'm not sure if that's a normal thing or it's just my family.*

When you're a teenager, you get into fashion and the whole trainer thing comes in, of buying Kickers and Adidas and Gola. Nowadays, now I'm in a different financial position, I think I have probably got too many shoes and trainers. In fact, I know I have, because Melanie and I counted them up the other day and I have thirty-two pairs. I know that's a bit silly, but in fairness to me, a lot are just ordinary black shoes. There's a reason for that. When I go on tour, I wear a suit and black shoes, and you would not believe the number of times I've turned up at gigs and forgotten to take shoes. I realise, *Shit, I've got to go and buy another pair of fucking black shoes!* I've literally got about eight pairs that are all the frigging same, so you could count them all as just being one pair.

Mind you, there's still room in my wardrobe for at least one more pair, because I'm trying to find a decent pair of vegan shoes. Having been a vegetarian for over thirty years, I don't like wearing leather. But I haven't found any decent vegan shoes yet. I'm still looking.

I suppose I've gone through different stages of clothes-buying in my life to date. In a funny way, I grew old quickly, because I was in Marks & Spencer suits in my twenties, when I was doing the pharmaceutical job. Then I got into stand-up and went through all that caper of trying to get a showbiz suit. Now I'm kind of back to normal suits again. The truth is, like most middle-aged blokes, I don't think about buying clothes all that much. I buy my own shoes, but other than that, I'm often just wearing things that my family have given me as presents. I guess that means that like all dads I am handing over a huge responsibility to my family because they could make me look shit. In fact that is the best excuse for wearing anything that looks a bit shit: put on a pained smile and just say 'it was a present'.

Just Say 'Yes! Yes! Yes!'

A lucky aspect of my job is that people give me free stuff. I'll go to do a television show, walk into the dressing room and somebody will say, 'Look, we've got the choice of these three jumpers to put on.' I love that – and it's not just the fact that it's free. It's the fact that someone else has gone to the shop for me and chosen them for me, and that's great. They have saved me two days of angst, wondering what to wear on TV.

The first time I got offered cool free stuff, my working-class roots definitely kicked in. A mate of mine, Jodie, is in the music business and he had a contact at Nike who he introduced to me. Jodie used to get in all the bands and sort them out with Nike gear and Nike trainers and he said that he would do the same to me. It was like going for my Hong Kong suit all over again. Jodie told me, 'Go to this street in Soho and find a black door, No. 75. It's nondescript, a little doorway with no logos or anything. Knock, go upstairs and they'll sort you out.'

When I got there, I walked into a room with wall-to-wall cupboards that folded out into a whole cave of Nike gear.

'This is fantastic!' I said.

'Well, take what you want,' the guy told me.

'I don't want to take the piss, or anything …' I said.

'No, take what you want,' he repeated. 'When you've finished, we'll have it all downstairs in a bag for you.'

I just couldn't resist. I spent ages trying on trainers. In the end, I think I took nine pairs. I've never been asked back. I suppose the guy had meant, 'Take what you want, as long as it's two pairs'

– but I had that working-class poor lad thing of, *Fucking hell, I'll never get another go at this!* And I was right.

But everything changes as you get older. When I think about clothes now, the phrase I keep coming back to is 'age-appropriate'. I don't want to dress like a grandad, but I also don't want to commit the worst sin of all – dressing too young.

I want to dress like a fifty-two-year-old because there is a real element of tragedy about a middle-aged man dressing too young. He is fooling himself, and nobody else. He must be thinking, *If I dress like I've just got off a skateboard, people will look at me and think, 'Doesn't he look great?'* But, really, everyone is just looking at him and thinking: *What a bell-end!* I live in fear of looking like that and so I have transitioned into a more comfortable area of age-appropriate clothing. But this doesn't mean it's made choosing clothes easy. In fact, it's the opposite. It takes me ages to get ready to get out, and Melanie is always tutting and waiting for me, because *I just don't know what to put on*.

Like a lot of men my age, I'm in an area now where I don't know what's trendy and I don't know what makes me look too old. I'm in a zone where I don't want to 'look like a dad', even though that's what I am. I'm a bit like, 'Fucking hell, I want to put on a pullover, but I don't want to *look* like I'm wearing a pullover!'

It's such a dilemma. If I'm going to a rock gig, I want to look as if I'm going to a rock gig, and as if I'm *meant* to be at a rock gig. I don't want to look as if I'm picking somebody else up who has been to the rock gig. I might wear a band T-shirt, but it has to be iconic. It has to be a band that I might have actually listened to, like the Beatles or the Clash. But, me, in my fifties, walking around in a Libertines T-shirt, trying to look like I am Pete Doherty's mate – that is never going to work.

At my age, you're caught halfway between trying to dress to impress and dressing for comfort. My wardrobe has still got some things in it that I love but that I'd never dare to wear now. I've got a mad psychedelic shirt I bought in Bali in 1992 for 50p. I've got button-down denim shirts that don't fit anymore, but I keep them just in case they start fitting again. I know I will never wear those things again – but I can't throw them away.

That's a lot to do with my age, and my generation. When I was a kid, I wore things until they were worn out. I remember getting a yellow Fred Perry shirt, my first Fred Perry, when I was thirteen, and it was like getting a pass. It felt like somebody had said, 'You've got a Fred Perry shirt, so you're on your way to being cool!' I couldn't afford to follow it up with the Harrington jacket, or anything like that, but I wore that Fred Perry shirt to death. I wore it until it was threadbare.

It's different for my kids. They don't think like that and they don't wear things out. They're a disposable generation. But even today, at my age, I will buy something and find myself looking at it and thinking that it will probably still be an appropriate thing for me to wear in twenty years' time. It's daft because some clothes are a real commitment and I've kept them longer than I've kept some friends, probably because I find them more reliable. They won't let you down and their only reason for existing at all is to make you look good.

The generation before mine is even more like that. I remember a few years ago, my dad came to watch me host a Royal Variety

Performance. It was a black-tie job, so I told my dad, 'I need to get you a black-tie dinner suit.' My dad said, 'That's buying a whole new suit, isn't it?' I said yes, it was, and my dad replied, 'Look, lad, I'm never going to get my wear out of that!'

I loved that. I wasn't expecting my dad to say, 'Well, I've got a black-tie suit and dickie-bow now, I'd better start wearing it to go the shops with your mum, to get my wear out of it!' But I think that attitude is a lovely way of looking at things. And I think I've partly inherited it.

Melanie helps me out with clothes advice and yet, like all married men, I know this advice is sometimes based on convenience rather than well-thought-out research. There have been times in the past when I have asked Melanie to pick me up a T-shirt and she has come home with one from George in Asda. Now, regardless of the merits of the garment, this T-shirt was bought as an add-on to a grocery shopping list. The simple truth is that if you buy your clothes in the same place you buy your cabbage you are unlikely to be regarded as the most fashionable man in the room.

There is one major thing about my wardrobe that has changed lately. There was a period a while ago when, whenever I was having a clear-out of clothes, my teenage sons would be all over it. They'd be scrabbling through the things I was getting rid of, taking what they wanted. But I had a clear-out recently and this time they weren't bothered. They all said, 'I'm not interested in any of those things.' So that sweet spot has now ended. The only other people who wear clothes that I buy are ... people like me. People who are my age.

In terms of where I am at now, as a man trying to grow old gracefully, I suppose part of me is thinking, at what point do I stop wearing jeans? That will probably be my last vestige of youth, or of youthful clothing – when I start wearing slacks or chinos continuously. I have got some friends who have made that step already, and I definitely have more slacks and chinos in my wardrobe than I used to have. What's more, I am sitting here writing this now in a jumper that I think my dad would wear. Deep down, I am very happy about that.

Ask an Expert

With all these questions going around my head about what a fifty-two-year-old man should wear, I recently decided to go and see a man who can answer them – Dylan Jones, the editor of *GQ*. *GQ* is a very significant magazine in that it vastly influences what a certain kind of man chooses to wear. It started in 1931 as an American fashion-industry trade publication but became hugely popular among the general public. This was because, even back in the 1930s, when the male fashion industry was a choice between a double-breasted suit or a flat cap and donkey jacket, men still wanted to know what was the best.

Arriving in the UK in 1988, *GQ* has ever since been the magazine of choice for millions of men who at some time or other have been looking for some direction, including me (although whenever I have bought it, I have hidden it inside a copy of *Razzle* or *Readers' Wives* because I didn't want people to think I was weird and was too interested in clothes).

Dylan Jones has been the editor since 1999, and when I contacted him with my middle-aged clothes worries, he invited me into his offices in central London for a chat. Meeting the editor of *GQ* is like going on a first date: I must have got changed four times to try and look good.

I imagined I would meet him at *GQ* and be paraded past the critical eyes of the staff, who spend their whole life wearing fabulous clothes and writing about these fabulous clothes and the fabulous people who wear them. I had a vision of Dylan telling all his staff to stop what they were doing and look at the tragic specimen in front of them: a classic example of a middle-aged lost cause that they, the *GQ* staff, had to learn from because they have the power to save such a wretch like me.

Thankfully, that didn't happen. Instead, I was led through a busy but normal-looking office where the dominant colour was black and the style was unequivocally relaxed. Dylan's office has a glass wall that looks onto the area where the team put the magazine together. It is smart but not over-formal and we sat in a couple of armchairs in front of extra-large copy of *GQ* with Prince Harry on the cover.

Dylan is slim (although he admitted to me that he has 'exploded' since he turned fifty and his thirty-two inch waist went almost overnight to being thirty-eight). If I am honest, finding out that not even being the editor of a lifestyle magazine that presents its readership with a vision of perfection can save you from middle-aged spread was surprisingly reassuring. I have known Dylan for a number of years now and I have always liked him. He interviewed me on stage at Hay-on-Wye festival in 2014 about my autobiography *How Did All This Happen?* (it appears to be compulsory that my book titles begin with the word 'How') and his journalistic skills were apparent to me then as he had clearly read the book, dissected it and asked pertinent and challenging questions. It was good to turn the tables and interview him this time.

Despite Dylan's longstanding career at *GQ* in the male fashion industry, he is yet another middle-aged, heterosexual white man, to add to myself and the rest of this book's creative team. At least it gave him a natural understanding of my dilemma. Here is what we talked about:

Me: One problem I have found as I get older, Dylan, is that I don't know what to wear.

Dylan: Yes, but deciding is easier than it used to be. Look at you, sitting there. You're wearing chinos, you're wearing a structureless shirt, and you could have worn the same things at twenty-five. The problem is when you try too hard to dress like a twenty-five-year-old. In terms of what a middle-aged man shouldn't do, what a middle-aged man shouldn't do is try and look younger than he is. It is as simple as that.

Me: I'm like a lot of fellas. I go online, on Mr Porter, and buy a box of stuff. When it arrives, I pull it out and think, *There's no way I'm fitting in that, why did I buy that?* I've told Melanie, as soon as you log on, the site needs to ask you, '*How old are you? We will take you to the age-appropriate section.*' Because as well as looking great, you've got to look suitable.

Dylan: Well, the good thing nowadays is that mature customers can go into Comme des Garçons or Armani or Paul Smith and buy clothes in thirty-four to forty inch waists. The fit is very important. So many men try and do the Van Morrison thing — they are getting bigger so they wear smaller clothes, thinking that because they're tighter they're going to make you look thin. Instead, they make you look fatter.

Me: Van Morrison can do what he wants!

Dylan: Yes, because he's Van Morrison! But a lot of older guys try and wear skinny jeans and skinny jackets and they just look stupid. You've got to go with your body. You've got to be comfortable.

Me: Have things got easier for older men since you started editing *GQ*?

Dylan: Definitely. The biggest trend has been that there is more on offer. When I came into this industry, at twenty-four, you had Bond Street and Paul Smith and nothing else. Now there's everything. You can go out and you can spend a relatively small amount of money and look great. Uniqlo do brilliant clothes for fifteen-year-old guys and fifty-five-year-old guys.

There are a lot of men of our age now who aren't fashionistas and who don't follow fashion but who just want to buy nice clothes. They like to build up their wardrobe. I'll buy a blue shirt jacket because I don't have one but I'm not going to buy one every six months.

Me: The problem with my wardrobe, Dylan, is it's just full of *stuff*. I haven't got outfits: I've got *stuff*. And a lot of it is the same stuff.

Dylan: But that's what men do! I sometimes get asked, usually by very enthusiastic Asian journalists, 'What's your style regime?' And I say, 'I get up in the morning, I put on a blue suit and I walk to work.' And I do. I've got fifty blue suits. They're different types of blue but they are blue suits. Men are obviously more conservative dressers than women but I also think as you get older, you do become more conservative. Unless you're like Nicky Haslam and you try and look like Liam Gallagher.

If you go on holiday to Ibiza now and you see a fifty-year-old guy from the UK, he's going to be better dressed than he was ten, twenty or thirty years ago.

Me: You can still spot Brits abroad, though.

Dylan: Of course you can, and you go in the other direction because you don't ever want to see Brits abroad. But we're dressing better because we can do. You can go into Zara and buy a great pair of baggy white cargo pants for £45. Twenty years ago, they would have either cost £500, or been £20 and totally disgusting.

You can go to brilliant stores like Matches or Flannels who sell designer clothes in a very sophisticated environment but you don't feel like a fashionista when you go into one of their shops. It's just a nice place to shop.

Me: But there's that word you've used a couple of times: fashionista. I always feel that there are people in the fashion world who follow fashion, who set trends, and then there's the rest of us. And I've always felt that it's a world that *people like me* are not allowed into. You have to qualify to get into it.

Dylan: That's changed, John. Thirty years ago, people in the fashion industry were sniffy and they did look down upon people if they were wearing last season's clothes. It was pathetic but that was what the industry was like. Now everything has become far more egalitarian and people of all ages can have taste and aspire to quality.

But I think it all goes back to what I was saying earlier about men's ... not vanity, but men's interest now in looking better than they did years ago, is driven by their partners: wives, girlfriends, boyfriends, whatever. A few years ago, newspapers were running features asking, 'Are men too vain?' And I just thought, *I'm sure their partners don't think so*. It's great if they smell better and regularly buy new underwear. As a nation, I genuinely think men of all ages are better dressed now than they have ever been.

Me: Well, you say that, but I'd like to point out that *GQ*, at its Men of the Year award, twice awarded its Politician of the Year prize to one of the scruffiest politicians ever: Boris Johnson.

Dylan: Yes, hands up. Guilty. But to be honest, it's a very difficult prize to award at the moment, because who has wanted to celebrate politicians in Britain in the last two years? They are very low wattage.

Me: It's pretty hard to get wearing a suit wrong, isn't it? But Boris Johnson manages it.

Dylan: Well, you look at someone like Obama and think he looks cool, but he is cool for a variety of reasons. I don't actually care what politicians look like, although it can be a problem if they don't look like a statesman, like Michael Foot didn't and Boris doesn't. But on the other hand, I think politicians being too fastidious in the way they look sends the wrong message. You don't want them to look over-preening . . .

Me: Peacocking.

Dylan: Yes. Nobody likes a peacock.

Me: I don't think anybody will ever call me a peacock. So, Dylan, what are your top tips for men who don't know what to wear, in their fifties and beyond?

Dylan: I think it all comes down to simplicity. If you find things that you like, wear them. If people say things suit you, listen to them. If my wife says, 'That shirt really looks good on you,' I wear that shirt. Wear the jeans that suit you, wear the shirts that suit you: add a significant piece of jewellery or a significant jacket. It's about simplicity, and about being comfortable. If you're comfortable you're going to be more attractive to people than if you are walking around worrying how you look. If a guy is confident, you often don't even notice what he's wearing.

Me: That's a good point. There are some people who never look scruffy or never look untidy or never look like they've dressed wrong but you actually can't remember what they had on.

Dylan: And a lot of that has got to do with your physique. If the fashion industry has done anything to improve the way men look, it's in the way that they are taking care of their bodies. It's true we are in an age where narcissism is celebrated and vanity can go off in ridiculous extremes but I think, generally, men of all ages seem to take more care of themselves. Most guys I know go to the gym.

It's easier to go to a gym now than it's ever been before and even if you can't afford to go to the gym you can run, you can work out and that's good. And often I think that if you've got a good body, you're looking after yourself you can just wear a T-shirt and a pair of jeans you're going to look good. Eat less, drink less, exercise more, and you don't have to worry so much about clothes.

Me: I agree. You don't have to worry about the wrapping. And I think that is a very good thing.

As I walked away from the *GQ* office, I reflected on what Dylan had said.

1. Don't dress too young.
2. You don't always have to spend a fortune.
3. You are not Van Morrison so do not wear tighter clothes.
4. Give your clothes a chance by looking after the body underneath them.
5. Boris Johnson will never be Barack Obama.

The reality is that in talking with Dylan, I was talking to someone whose professional position meant that he had to be interested in fashion and clothes. My conclusion is that no matter how much I try, I simply don't care enough. I like feeling smart and within the slipstream of fashion but I will never lead the way.

A few years ago I had two tickets to go and see Billy Connolly live at the Hammersmith Apollo and I asked my son Luke if he wanted to come. Luke was living in London at the time and though he is not the biggest comedy fan, he knew that I am a big fan of Billy and he was happy to accompany me. When we met I noticed he had a skull ring on – not a small one but a large ring on his middle finger that looked like something a pirate would cut your hand off for. When I pointed it out he said, 'You should get one, Dad, you would look cool.'

I said, 'Luke at my age I wouldn't look cool, I would look ridiculous wearing a ring like that!'

We went the show which was great, and we were lucky enough to be invited backstage to see Billy. I had met Billy on a few occasions in the past and though he is always gracious and friendly, I always try not to overstay my welcome because I know sometimes after a show you can feel tired. I would imagine even more so if you are a man in your seventies who has just done two and half hours comedy, without an interval, to an adoring crowd. But as soon as we walked in Billy's face lit up and as soon as I introduced Luke they bonded.

'I love the ring,' said Billy, immediately putting his fist forward to show he was wearing a skull ring equal in size to Luke's.

The lesson I took from that was that you are never too old to wear something that is cool, provided you start off by being as cool as Billy Connolly. I still haven't got a skull ring and I am not sure I will ever be that cool.

3.

HOW TO BE A FAMILY MAN

THERE IS A VERY good reason why we use the expression 'a family man' rather than 'a man who has a family'. It's because once you acquire a partner and children, you sacrifice your individuality. The family come first. Even in this age of gender equality, there is no equivalent expression of 'a family woman' but being called 'a family man' effectively defines your priority in life.

In fact, if you are introduced as a family man you have already set out your stall. When somebody is described as a family man, you don't think, Great, I bet *he* was clubbing till five in the morning, rides a Harley-Davidson and has the tattoo of a stripper he once met in Hamburg on his arm. Instead, you think of a man in a polo shirt, wearing slacks, smiling through adversity while trying to keep his head above water in a job he hates in lower middle-management, where his dwindling career prospects are so low that he hopes nobody notices how bad he is at his job before he qualifies for his pension.

Nobody says the words 'family man' to create a frisson of excitement about the person who you are talking about. The phrase is the verbal equivalent of an anorak – it describes something that has a function. All that you want is for it to do its job when called upon and nothing else. You don't need an anorak when the sun is out, and the family don't need *you* when everything is going well. In fact, it might be fair to say that a testament to how well a family is doing is based on how involved the dad is. If he is involved in everything, then everything must be a bit shit.

Being a family man has been the most rewarding and the most disappointing thing I have done in my life. I am sure I am not alone in feeling that. I have worked hard to be all the things that I thought a family man should be, but I am sad to say that in a number of areas I probably could have done better by not trying to run a family like I was picking a five-a-side football team.

To become a family man, the first thing you need is a partner or, as I would call it, a 'team captain'. Melanie became my team captain and, once she was signed up, things started happening. We had our oldest son, Joe, fourteen months after we got married. We had both wanted children early but perhaps not quite as soon as that. As our first signing, the arrival of Joe promoted me from just being a married man to being a 'family man', with all the inherent joys and pressures that brings. A married man can still have a glint in his eye and a spring in his step because he is forbidden fruit. A family man generally has sleep in his eye and smells of rotten fruit from sick on his shoulder from the baby rejecting some form of puréed food.

Joe, Melanie and I were now a team. However, because that development had come quicker that we envisaged, we had not fully worked on our formation and style of play before my accuracy and Melanie's fertility meant that we expanded the squad when Luke arrived eighteen months after Joe. As a family formation, this worked perfectly. Obviously, some would say that the best line-up in a family formation of four is one boy and one girl to give balance, like a right-footer and a left-footer in football. Melanie and I did discuss the fact that having a daughter would be a good thing to complete the team/family ... but, twenty months later, Daniel arrived.

This was fine. We were not disappointed to have another son and, in many ways, we were both relieved that he arrived alone because we knew we were gambling with every new addition as my dad is a twin and producing twins can be genetic. Melanie and I agreed that if we went on searching for that elusive daughter after Daniel, and instead had two more boys at once, it would be a disaster. It would complete our five-a-side team but it would make the squad too big to keep everybody happy – particularly the management team. Five boys would simply be too many to handle. Getting that many children to move in one direction requires a lot of shouting, a cattle prod and a sheep dog. I would stop being a family man and would have become a shepherd.

Upon Daniel's arrival the natural balance of the squad was altered anyway, because the world is not set up for families of more than four. Nature itself sends you the message that two children is enough by only providing you with two hands. If you have three children under the age of four, as I did, you have to make choices, because you cannot hold hands with all of them.

It is a bit easier when you have a pram. We had a double buggy that had served a purpose for Joe and Luke. When Dan arrived, it became his buggy, and Luke and Joe would stand on the kickboard at the back and ride it like a husky sledge. This way I could transport all of them in one go and ensure they were all going in the same direction. However, once they all grew too big for the pram and wanted to walk, nature's message was loud and clear: you have to pick which two you want hold hands with, and which one you are prepared to take a gamble with.

Logic would suggest that the oldest child should be allowed to walk alongside you and would not need his hand holding as much as his younger brothers. However, that assumption does not take into account the adventurous nature of boys, who instinctively seem to feel that if they are not tethered or bound to something, they are free to roam the earth in whichever direction they please, as if the world were one giant soft play area and their parent will not be frantic if they have lost sight of you for thirty seconds. No sight should incite sympathy more than an overwhelmed parent holding hands with two children while trying to herd the rest of their offspring with their feet. They are like a juggler who has been thrown too many balls and at any moment is likely to drop the lot.

For a while, I used the invention that best symbolises the modern father – a papoose. These things were *definitely* not around when I was a baby, and if they had been, I am not sure if I can envisage my father's generation taking to them as well as we have. I am not trying for one minute to suggest that the generation before us didn't engage with their children, but let's just say that the expectations were different. If my dad took me to the pub, I sat in the car outside with a packet of crisps and a bottle of lemonade, pretending to drive the unlocked car, while he had a few pints with his mates.

By contrast, if I took any of my young lads to the pub, it had to be a child-friendly pub with a ball pool, where I could sit and possibly get a coffee while hoping my boy did not knock over any other kids as he manically ran around flushed with the after-effects of his fortified sugary drink. You can tell a lot about parents at these children's play areas. There are the worriers like me, who are constantly checking their child is not being injured by another child, is not injuring another child, is not being bullied, is not bullying and is asking them every few minutes if they need the toilet.

There are the other kind of parents who sit reading a paper, chatting on the phone and drinking a bottle of wine as if they're enjoying an afternoon out on holiday. These other parents somehow manage to block out the noise of dozens of screaming kids around them. I don't want to imply that these stress-free parents were *always* dressed in leggings or tracksuits, but there was definitely a strong correlation between casual leisurewear, a high BMI index and a laissez-faire attitude to child safety. It may sound as if I am knocking these people, but I am not: I always wished I was more like them. The ability to chill out and relax while your child could bang heads with another child at any minute was one that I always envied. Even to this day I worry about my sons; in fact, Joe is twenty-five, Luke is twenty-three and Daniel is twenty-one and I have worried about each of them every day since they were born. As their accumulated age is sixty-nine I have worried about them for longer than I have been alive.

My dad was of the generation that would smoke a roll-up cigarette while putting petrol into a car full of children without a second thought. He never saw any of his kids being born. That sort of thing was not encouraged in the 1960s. Instead, his job was to wait in the corridor of the hospital, smoking, as the midwife delivered his new baby, washed it and presented it to him like a prize, all dressed, cleaned and happy.

My generation are the neurotic ones who are constantly hoping they are doing the right thing and praying that nothing goes wrong due to their lack of parenting skills. Therapists' offices all over the world are full of patients blaming their parents for their own failings. Well, it is true that there are *abusive* parents out there, but the majority of us are simply doing the best we can. Until you become a parent you don't realise what you don't know, and the truth is you don't know anything.

The Parent Test

It is one of the ultimate life lessons. Until you assume the lifelong responsibility for the wellbeing of another human being, it is impossible to understand what being a parent is. There is no check list, no annual appraisal, and no way of knowing if you are doing it right until it is too late to correct the mistakes you make. A child is like an unhatched egg. You tend to it the best you can, you place it in the best places for it to be taken care of and to grow, and then one day that egg hatches, an adult walks out, and all the decisions and inputs that you made are stood in front of you in their full-grown glory.

There is no greater heartbreak than to think you may have let your own child down: to think that a different school would have been better, or you should have made them continue with that club or after-school activity, or just you could have been *more present*. Hindsight is a pernicious thing, and when it comes to parenting the hindsight is stood in front of you, wearing a hoodie, asking you for money.

As your kids grow up, there is a natural tendency to live vicariously through them, which is totally understandable. From the day they were born you have wanted the best for them, often to the detriment of yourself. You can make up for the things you had to walk away from by trying to ensure that your kids take every opportunity that is put in front of them.

I read an article the other week about a couple who said that having a dog was like having a child. *No. It's not.* You will never move to a new house to get the dog into a good school. You have total control over where the dog goes and what other dogs it sees and you never worry what influences the dog is getting from other dogs on the internet. The dog will never ask for a smartphone or iPad, will never answer back, will never start smoking, and will never be delivered back to you in a wheelbarrow, worse for wear after its first experience of drinking. A dog only wants to make you happy and expects nothing in return. There are no mood swings, no real acts of defiance, and no meetings with headmasters to discuss the dog's behaviour.*

I have three dogs: two English bull terriers, Bilko and Tigger, and one tiny creature of indeterminate breed, called Alfie, inherited from Melanie's mum, who is best described as a real dog but smaller. They are all rescue dogs because, apart from making your own children if you are able to do so, I don't see the need for something to be bred to join your family. There are loads of dogs' homes with good dogs needing a home, so going to a breeder and spending money has never made any sense to me, particularly considering some of the horrendous stories about puppy farms.

One argument against rescue dogs is that you don't know their history and so you don't know if you are inheriting a problem.

---

* *Having said that, I stopped picking up my kids' shit not long after they were born. I am still doing it for the dogs, and one of them is fifteen.*

But I think if you get to spend time with a dog you can learn a lot about it quickly and can educate it to live with your family in the way you want.

I say all of this with the caveat that the gap between aspiration and reality in the behaviour of dogs and children is often the same. One of our dogs, Tigger, is the laziest dog in the world. Everybody knows that all dogs like a walk. Not Tigger. Anyone who sees me taking my dogs for a walk will invariably witness Alfie and Bilko running on ahead of me while I struggle behind them, dragging Tigger along by the harness.

Dogs have much less complicated brains than children. They have fewer reasons to try and enforce their will or to go against yours. Despite this, in the six years we have had Tigger, she has always insisted on sitting down within the first fifty yards of a walk and forcing whoever is walking her into a dragging contest.

It is exactly the same with children. You can sign them up for the Cubs, for Sea Cadets, for after-school clubs, for sports teams, for drama and dance classes, for music lessons, for adventure holidays, for the Duke of Edinburgh Awards and for a million things that you wished someone had signed you up for when you were a kid, and they can refuse to go to them without giving a second thought to the opportunity lost. They don't see it as an opportunity lost but as a simple decision between one activity and another. If the other one is playing *FIFA* on an Xbox, it doesn't even register with them that, in the long run, playing *FIFA* on an Xbox might be less rewarding than learning to abseil or play the clarinet.

I suppose that what I am basically saying is that what you learn as you get older is that being a parent is bloody hard. The bits that you get right go unnoticed, and the bits you get wrong live with you forever, even if they are not entirely your fault. Unwilling children may be like unwilling English bull terriers but it is simply not socially acceptable to put a lead on them and drag them to the Cubs or Sea Scouts, much as you would like to do so.

Being Married

Inherent in the title of 'a family man' is the fact that the family must remain intact. Otherwise you become a 'divorced man' and that is a very different beast indeed. If a bachelor is like an Olympic sprinter ready to race for the prize, be it to sleep with the next single girl he meets, chase his next selfish high or simply hang out with his other single friends and enjoy all the freedoms afforded to him from his bachelor status, then a divorced man is like a sprinter with a limp.

A divorced man has a status that will always need explaining. You can't be divorced, meet someone new, and not be asked questions about the life choices that brought you to being a divorced man. A bachelor never has to explain anything. You are a bachelor because you have not yet made the commitment to becoming a married, family or divorced man, but the world assumes it is only a matter of time. Being a bachelor brings with it fewer expectations than those other states: you are simply young, free and single.

The etymology of bachelor is interesting. The word itself is derived from the twelfth-century 'knight bachelor', who was a young knight too poor or too young to 'gather vassals under their own banner'. This meant they could own some land but not have people pledge allegiance to them – in fact, they themselves had to pledge allegiance to a feudal lord and operate under their banner. Thus, throughout history, the term 'bachelor' has been used to symbolise someone who has yet to reach their full potential.

By contrast, the term 'married man' indicates that that man has at least reached the position in life where they are good enough to attract a mate. A 'family man' is a step on again: somebody who has everything sorted, or at least so the world assumes. If you are a divorced man, the world knows that everything has gone tits up.

If you are expecting any more wisdom from me here about how to maintain a family, I am afraid I have no magic to offer. I am not the best father in the world and I am not the best husband either. However, I do love my family, in a way that can sometimes feel frightening because, for all of my failings as a family man, I know that it is the only thing in life that is actually truly important to me.

I have been married to Melanie since 29 May 1993. We had two years apart when the pressures of being young parents of three children, all born within three and half years, plus demanding jobs meant that we imploded and split up. I have often spoken about this period and it is well documented that this was when I started doing stand-up comedy. Thankfully, after numerous sessions at Relate, Melanie and I managed to see that being together was better for us all than being apart. To me, this is the essence of being a 'family' man: being part of something that is better with you being there and which makes you better, even if you sometimes don't realise it.

Being a parent is a challenge for anyone but there is a special factor in being the father of boys. You have to make them tough enough not to need you, even though you hate the moment when they don't need you. All fathers of sons will have to face the day that your son holds your hand for the very last time and will never hold it again. When you think about it, it's heart-breaking, particularly considering that it passes without either of you knowing, and so without comment. There is no declaration that a milestone has been passed, like when they are allowed to have their first sleepover or to make their own way home from school for the first time. It just ends, and it never happens again.

Eventually, fathers and sons have to push each other away. It's nature's way and it is what society expects. My three sons are now young men in their early twenties, and if I was walking down the street holding hands with them, either it would look as if I were grooming them or they would look like my carers. It would look odd either way – but it is still a profound sadness that it has to happen.

As you get older, you understand that being a parent is not only the most important job in the world, but it's also the hardest. The world that you used to live in no longer exists and you are charged with guiding your offspring through a terrain you have never walked on yourself. There is simply too much information out there to be on top of. Eric Schmidt, the CEO of Google, said in 2010, 'There were five exabytes of information created in the entire world between the dawn of civilisation and 2003. Now the same amount is created every two days.' My world is much closer to the world that my parents lived in than the one my kids now inhabit of the internet and mass mobile communication

Then again, maybe that is what the parents of every generation have always felt like. The world is constantly changing and the way you try to guide your children through it constantly changes. Perhaps every generation feels the one above them doesn't understand them, and the one below them is simply entitled and living off the hard work of their predecessors.

The big question is this: if the most important aspect of being a family man is being a father, how can you be the best father you can? Again, I don't have any easy answers, because when you are a parent you never know if you are doing the right thing. Obviously, if by the time your child is in its teens, they are representing the country at sport, achieving five A*s in their A levels and picking between university scholarship offers, while also balancing acting, singing and modelling careers, the chances are you have done a decent job. However, for most of us, being a parent is like living in a power cut. You just head to whatever light you can see.

We had our three sons in just over three years between 1994 and 1998. I was twenty-seven when the first one arrived. I realised at the time that I had got married and become a father earlier than most of my contemporaries, but I guess my life expectations had inevitably been influenced by my parents. They were married when they were still teenagers and had already had four children by their early twenties. But you can't plan these things methodically – they are influenced by so many random factors, primarily meeting the person you want to be with.

Meeting Melanie changed everything for me. I knew I wanted to be with her. That meant getting married and everything else just followed on. However, I think it is fair to say that I was in too much of a rush to grow up. As this is a book about growing old, I think the one thing I would have said to my younger self is this: 'Slow down a bit. You don't need the wife, house, car, children and dog so soon. Spend a few summers in Ibiza, or on a kibbutz.'

I still tell myself this nowadays. Not that I should go to Ibiza or a kibbutz, but that I should relax a bit more. Progress in life sometimes happens when you appear to be doing nothing but being still. That may sound very New Age and hippy-ish but it's a truth I am only just learning: *Sometimes, by doing nothing, you are doing everything.* I bet somebody, somewhere has that as a tattoo. Probably in Goa.

The Generation Gap

It would appear that this is not a lesson that our children have to learn. The generation which came after mine, called Generation Y but more widely known as millennials, has significantly different life expectations. In a 2017 survey of 2,000 millennials – people born between 1980 and 2000 – by the Nationwide Building Society, the majority did not consider themselves to be 'grown up' until they were at least twenty-seven. Speaking as somebody who was already married with a mortgage and a child by then, I think they are probably right. Considering we are probably all going to work until the day before we pop off, around aged eighty, I think that my generation probably grew up a little too quickly.

Sociologists call my generation – people born between 1966 and 1979 – Generation X. Before us came the baby boomers, born between 1946 and 1965. They were the generation that enjoyed massive social change, sexual liberation, enhanced social mobility and the benefits of a welfare state. Not to mention home ownership, foreign travel on a scale their parents would never have dreamed of, and a more secure employment environment than their parents, due to government subsidies and nationalisation within many business sectors. The baby boomers did very nicely. In 2004, they held 80 per cent of the wealth in the UK, they bought 80 per cent of the top-of-the-range cars and 80 per cent of all cruises, and –

surprisingly – purchased 50 per cent of all skin-care products. I say surprisingly because when you look at the state of a lot of them, they must have bought them as gifts for other people.

It is surprising, then, that baby boomers were the biggest demographic that voted to leave the European Union in the Brexit referendum. This has naturally angered millennials, who see the baby boomers as the generation who already had the best of everything. To my sons' generation, they are like the neighbours who come to your house party, eat and drink everything, and then piss off just before the end to go home and call the police to complain about the noise. However, they are the generation with some of the most progressive thinkers ever. When there was a cross-generational conversation about Brexit in our house, involving me, Melanie, her mum Eileen and our son Joe – something that must have been happening all over the country in recent years – Joe suggested that his generation will lose out because Eileen's one swung the vote to Brexit. Eileen's response was that whatever the merits of the vote, her generation gave us the Beatles, so they had made their contribution to making the world a better place. To be fair, it was a convincing argument.

I have a theory that the main reason why those born from the late 1990s onwards see the world so differently from my generation is because all their lives they have been able to *see the world*. It may be through the filter of the internet and social media, but at any given moment, on any given day, they can log on and plug into the world and see what is happening. My generation didn't have that option. For us to gain an understanding of the world, we had to physically go and see it. Late-millennials/Gen Z have always known they can pick up their mobile phones and the world is at their fingertips.

I know my theory is slightly over-simplified, but let me give you an example. While writing this chapter, I have FaceTimed one of my sons, who is on holiday in Majorca. I saw him on a screen, in my hand, and had a conversation with him. An hour earlier, I spoke with his brother, who is in Madrid on a course, and last night I spoke to the third one, who is travelling in Thailand.

I had all of these conversations within twenty-four hours. If I want another, I can contact any of them within seconds. It's a far cry from when I was young, and it is technology that has made the world so much smaller for them, and so much easier to go off and do those things. I still have a letter that my dad wrote to me when I first left home and went to Newcastle to study. I know my parents still have postcards I sent them when I was travelling in 1992. Back then, phoning home from abroad was regarded as excessive. Speaking on a video call? That belonged to science fiction but for my children's generation this is the new normal. It is like professional footballers wearing yellow football boots; I don't think anyone in my generation can understand it but my kids don't know a world where this didn't happen.

Empty Nesting

There is an inevitable end to the process of being a family man. Your children grow up, leave home, and you spend your time trying to think of reasons to call them. As our boys all arrived so close together, they also left home close together, and Melanie and I were left to cope with what is known as empty-nest syndrome. It's not easy.

The first night you and your partner are sat in the house after the last child fills a bag and leaves is very strange. You find yourself looking at each other as if to say, *Well, what now?* All of your energies have gone into reaching this point, and now that it has arrived you don't know what to say because, for the first time in longer than you can remember, there is just you two.

The common enemy – the children – has left, and with them so has the common theme for 90 per cent of your conversations and the glue that has held you together in your common pursuit. When they leave, it's inevitable that you and your partner will look at each other and ask, *Well, do you want to carry on or just call it quits?*

Melanie tried to cope with empty nesting by filling the nest with rescue animals. In addition to our three dogs we now have four horses, two Shetland ponies, chickens, sheep, geese, turkeys and two female pigs who live in the same area as the chickens. We also have a male pot-bellied pig called Milo who basically goes wherever he wants. He has now decided he is a horse and so lives in the stables with the horses. The animals have been a great distraction. Without them, I am not sure how we would have coped with the boys leaving.

As the boys have all moved to London, we moved house to be closer to them. They are part of the boomerang generation, the adult children who leave then come back home to live. They have all, at different points, moved back home for a month or so while they have been looking for a new flat or job. However, it does not alter the basic fact that they have all left home and will never live permanently in our home again.

We are maybe still a bit in denial about this, though, as Melanie has allocated each of them their own room in our new house.

They all have a room with some of their things in. I try to say that all of those rooms are spare rooms but, in my heart, I *like* the fact that Daniel, Luke and Joe still have their own spaces in the family home.

Despite this, it's still the ultimate mid-life rite of passage. We know we will never get the chance to be parents again in the way that we were. I will never get to sit on a couch and have all three boys draped over me while we watch TV. Melanie will never have another Mother's Day card painted in school lessons and brought home to hang on the fridge.

I can't deny that we miss it. I would give everything I own for just one day where I could pretend to be a horse and have them all ride together on my back again. I'd even love to be there again as they navigated the dark avenues of the teenage years into manhood. But I can't. That time is passed. Today, being a family man means waiting for them to come and visit, and hoping that we all get on well – because it's not easy telling a bloke in his twenties, who is bigger than you, to go to his room.

But one thing I think our generation should thank my son's generation for is the fact that they are more open with their feelings. When I speak to any of them on the phone we all finish the call by saying 'Love you!' I have not said that enough to my own parents and I could never say it too much to my own family, because the essence of being a family man is held in those two words, and having someone to say them to.

4.

HOW TO BE A FRIEND

'Friendship is the hardest thing in the world to explain. But if you haven't learned the meaning of friendship, you really haven't learnt anything.'

Muhammad Ali

ONE OF THE BIGGEST changes as you grow older is the fact that everybody around you grows older as well. That may seem an obvious thing to say but it impacts on the relationships you have and the new ones that you can develop. Some friendships seem stuck in the time they were born. If you are not sure what I mean by this, just watch middle-aged men hold a student reunion. There is nothing more inappropriate than men in their fifties laughing at farts in the same way they did when they were eighteen.

I am not saying farts are not funny but it is all about context. When you are eighteen, a fart is the funniest thing ever. As students we would announce a fart's arrival, and all the occupants of our student house would gather round for the event. Even better was going to the extent of using a lighter to light the methane for ultimate hilarity. This is because when you are eighteen you know when you are going to fart: it's not easy to do this in your fifties, when you can't announce the arrival of a fart you don't even know is going to happen. An oft-missed landmark on the journey to old age is the point where you can no longer control your flatulence.

I never thought I would be surprised by my own farts. Now I reach for a book, and a fart falls out. I can be walking and hear a noise, even before I feel the slight buttocks-wobble that tells me I have dropped one. At times, I have heard the tell-tale sound, felt no wobble and turned around to see I am alone. Instead of farts being a source of illicit, childish fun, in middle age they become an example of the philosophical question: if a tree falls in a forest and nobody is there to hear it, does it make a sound? The equivalent question is: if a fart enters a room and nobody knows where it came from, is it anyone's fault? Nothing makes you feel old more than realising that you can now fart in ignorance because your buttocks are so loose. They are like a set of open curtains that wind can pass through without even ruffling them.

As you grow older and become a victim of the unintended stealth fart, you learn to adopt the 'I dare you to say something' face. I have often been interacting with people, such as being served in a shop or ordering a drink, and my arse has decided to fart without giving me any advance warning. This means that both I and the person I am talking to are surprised by the sudden noise. My arse has not given me notice to adopt the social clench where my sphincter is like a balloon that has two fingers at its neck trying desperately not to let any of the air out.

On these occasions, I style it out and simply adopt my 'I dare you to say something' face. This blank expression makes the other person question what went on. If they are young, they would have the same instinctive reaction to a fart as did I at eighteen – they will want to laugh. However, if I am staring at them without even a hint of a smirk, they will start to question if they heard a fart at all.[*]

Though I have learnt this technique to avoid social embarrassment, it does answer the tree-in-the-forest question. If the person you are talking to does not immediately ask you, 'Did you just fart?', the moment passes. There is a tiny window of opportunity to ask this question. At the time, it is appropriate. Calling someone up a few hours later and inquiring, 'Did you drop one when we were talking today?' would seem weird, to say the least, so once that moment has gone, it is like it never happened.

If it has not been given a name, title or a place in the world, then the orphan fart is left to evaporate as if it were never there. The other person is left uncertain if they even heard anything at all. You just have to hold your face and give nothing away in your eyes as even the slightest flicker will betray your secret. It is a high-stakes social bluff but it is so much better than the other option of owning up mid-sentence: *'Hi, I will have the lasagne [FART!] … Oh, I am sorry, that is a fart that just fell out of my arse without warning! I do apologise. I didn't know it was coming but, don't worry, there is a never a follow-through. It's just my arse is looser than it used to be … oh, and can I have some olives and garlic bread as well, please?'*

If it stinks then all bets are off. That is why I believe old people always go everywhere with their dogs. At least if there is a pet

---

[*] *If the other person is a similar age to me, it is slightly easier. If I give nothing away to suggest it was me, they automatically think it was probably them.*

there, they can glance towards him with apologetic eyes that say, *I'm sorry my dog stinks, but he is great company, and I just hope I die before him because if he goes first I won't be able to cope with the loss and the loneliness. So please don't say anything about the smell because he is all I have in the world.*

Middle-aged men getting together will laugh at farts as they did in their youth not because they are trying to recapture those halcyon days but because it is only among friends that you can relax. And once you relax, all the tension of holding in the gas you couldn't let escape in job interviews, intimate sexual moments, career appraisals, mortgage applications, parents' evenings, weddings, christenings, funerals, doctor's appointments, haircuts, spa weekends, family dinners, school pick-ups and the millions of other moments where you could not be seen to let the side down, all that tension has gone and you can fart without social judgement. Among your mates, what would in other situations be a social stigma instead becomes a badge of honour.

Different Kinds of Friends

Friendships change in more ways than just farting. The older you get the more complicated your relationships become and you make friends in different circumstances. Work presents an obvious opportunity as you have enough in common with your colleagues to be at the same place every day. However, as you grow older your position in work changes. Nobody wants to be the sad, David Brent-like bloke who doesn't realise that, at your age, hanging around with the work interns is creepy and weird, and also that team bonding should not under any circumstances involve you taking your shirt off.

If you are married, you find that it's simply easier to develop new relationships with other couples. At least then, as you all grow older, when one of them dies you will still have one friend between you. It is also true that as you take steps into middle age, you have to push yourself to make new friends – particularly if you're a man. By this age, the natural instinct is to hold onto to what you know and not step outside of your comfort zone. That is very much what I am like. Despite really enjoying people's company, I have been lazy when it comes to friendships and could easily drift into grumpy old age. I am determined not to do so.

The passage of time means that your friendship groups inevitably evolve. This is partly through circumstance, partly through geography as people's lives change and they move away, and partly through laziness. It is simply too hard to maintain old relationships so it may be better to start new ones ... or, if you are like me, not bother at all.

Friendship for men seems to be an entirely different thing than it is for women. Men have *mates* but women have *friends*. It's a genuine difference. Melanie has some new friends that she has met in recent years but she also has her best friends who have been there since she was a teenager. I just have some new mates and some old mates.

I am being slightly dismissive here. Within both groups I have proper friends – but 'friends' is a title that men find harder to attribute than women seem to. It may be simply a question of vocabulary, or possibly a more deep-seated issue in the male psychology (though I think this is now slowly changing as men get more open about their feelings and talking to each other). You don't spend large parts of your time with people purely because one of you may fart and give you all something to laugh at. Despite how it may sometimes seem, most male relationships go a lot deeper than that.

Eventually you recognise that you are spending time with your mates for more reasons than just to talk about tits and football and drink beer. Our growing awareness of male mental health is all tied up in how we allow ourselves to be with each other as men. Like many men of my age, I have sadly known, both directly and indirectly, the awful consequences of men feeling unable to talk about their issues and instead choosing to take their own life.

The Price of Silence

Male suicide rates in the UK make for stark reading. Suicide is the most common cause of death for men in England and Wales between the ages of 20 and 49. There were 5,821 suicides in Britain in 2017 and 75 per cent of them were men. About 12 men per day take their own lives. The highest age-specific rate is 24.8 per 100,000 among men aged 45–49. It is clear there is a male issue here – and so-called mid-life crises can actually develop into life-ending meltdowns.

I have a friend who works for the Samaritans. This is an activity that has changed him and turned a really good man into someone truly special. The Samaritans are a brilliant organisation but, prior to my mate working there, and like a lot of people, I was ignorant of some of the work that they do. The Samaritans are not allowed to give advice to the desperate people on the other end of the line. They are simply there to offer emotional support and to explore the callers' feelings when people are struggling to cope, whether it be day or night.

This can even include sitting on the phone and listening as somebody contemplates committing suicide. They have listening techniques to help try and make the suicidal person on the line think about what they are doing and explore their options, but their remit does not allow them to try to talk them out of it – or even to call the authorities, unless there is a safeguarding issue.

What my friend has told me is that many of the suicidal people phone in not because they want to have their minds changed but because they don't want to be totally alone in their last moments of life. I must admit, I can't imagine the depth of humanity you must have in your soul to volunteer to be a Samaritan, knowing that on any shift you may be asked to sit on the phone and listen while someone you don't know takes their own life and your role is not to try and save them from this decision but to give them the final comfort of not being alone.

The need for comfort at the end of life, even when you have chosen to take your own life, was starkly illustrated to me when I was on tour in Dublin and met someone who worked on the Dart, the electric train that is the quickest way to get around Dublin and which extends out to County Wicklow. Part of his remit was to ensure the drivers who were at the controls when someone committed suicide by standing in front of the train received the full support they required. In doing this he has heard many of the stories of what the drivers saw and experienced as the person stepped onto the track. The thing that left a lasting impression on him, and me once he told me, was the fact that more than 50 per cent of the drivers said that the victim was stood looking directly at the oncoming train, while sucking their thumb.

To be unable to prevent your train from hitting an adult standing in front of you, doing what all children in the world do as they transition from their mother's breast into the brutal world where comfort is much harder to find, that must be an image that burns onto your brain like battery acid. Adults don't suck their thumbs: societal norms took that comfort away from them a long time ago. Yet in their final seconds, as they stand alone facing death, they instinctively crave that comfort again.

Stories like this have taught me that maybe some of the 5,821 people we lost in the UK in 2017 needed a friend and that might have been enough to stop them falling into the abyss that led to suicide. I know there are other factors. I'm sure it is no coincidence that the highest rate of male suicide per age correlates exactly with the most popular age for divorce: 45–49. I think it is also fair to say that, as middle age sees the highest suicide rate for both sexes, it also reflects that some people are not living the lives that they had imagined for themselves and are not seeing much opportunity in their declining years to make things better.

Mental health, debt and family pressure all play a part, but I can't help feeling that loneliness is the heaviest weight that can be placed on anybody. Feeling nobody cares about you and that you don't matter is something that we have all felt, at different times, to a greater or lesser extent, but when it is part of your daily life, I don't see how you can lift that cloud without the help of others. Friendship isn't a bonus in life: it is the single greatest nutrient we need if we are to avoid being one day sat on the end of a phone, hoping a stranger will stay with us.

Finding Friends

Men seem to acquire friends in the same way that we acquire tattoos. We collect them in our late teens and early twenties, then spend half our life regretting some of our decisions and wondering how to get rid of them. We often accept that it's more painful to get rid of them than to keep them – just as long as we're not seen with them out in certain situations.

There is a lot of research that illustrates the importance of friendship and interaction with others as we grow older: the worst thing that can happen to anyone is to be old and alone. However, to avoid that you have to keep your friendships fertile by working at them – and, let's be honest, at times it all just seems a bit too much time and effort. When we are all busy with family, work and life in general, that mate at university whom you carried home when he wet his pants and passed out on your floor thirty years ago may seem more trouble than he's worth. But if you have kept in touch all that time, there has to be *something* there.

I found the Muhammed Ali quote at the start of this chapter when I Googled 'quotes about friendship'. That's the thing: we now live in a world where it's possible to look very clever very quickly by going online and Googling without ever having to read a book. Yet doing something like Googling quotes about friendship is a great way of investigating what friendship means to you. It is amazing how many people have said something about it, which just shows how important friendship is to people.

And Muhammad Ali was right. Friendship *is* difficult to explain, particularly when I look at my own friendship group. I'm no different from any other man in his fifties who will have a group of mates, within which there will always be one or two that you keep on wondering why you are friends with them, and why they are friends with you, because you appear to have nothing in common. But then you get together and the unique gel that makes friendship so important and empowering is suddenly apparent.

When you are growing up, friendships all grow out of the situation you are in. Mostly, this is out of your hands. Not many children pick the school they go to, they don't pick the place they live and, until they reach a certain age, they hardly even pick the activities they engage in. As you reach maturity, however, that's when you begin to select the friends who will be around potentially for the rest of your life – that is a huge responsibility to place on somebody else and on yourself.

You don't know this at the time. Your new friend might just be the first person you meet at your hall of residence when you go to university. It might be the first person in your new job that got your joke. It might even be the mate of a mate, who you grow to find that you have more in common with than either of you do with your mutual friend, creating the awkward dilemma of seeing each other without your original mate, which feels like you're having an affair. There is a quote from C.S. Lewis's *The Four Loves* that I think is very apt: 'Friendship is born the moment that one person says to another, "You too? I thought I was the only one!"'

Anti-Social Media

With the advent of social media and mobile phones, the nature of friendship has changed massively. Nowadays, I have a Facebook account that I hardly look at, an Instagram account which I use for fun but also for work, and a Twitter account that I also use for work, but primarily to vent fury at politicians and celebrate football results. Because of the nature of my job, I see all of these as vehicles for communicating in relation to my work, but I know many people see them as mainly a vehicle for communicating with friends (even if those friends may actually be robots, somewhere within a cyber-factory in Russia, feeding you false information about American presidential elections).

If you are not in the public eye then the likelihood is that any social activity you engage in will be with your family or friends. I can see the benefits of this, but it is inevitable that it will also give you a window into the world of other people who present themselves as having faultless lives.

This practice is a downside to social media. I suppose I am in a relatively privileged position in life, yet I can still be negatively affected by posts. Even famous people who I know do not have perfect lives can post things that make it look like everything is perfect, or certainly at the moment in time they appear to be winning at life. This makes me feel that, by contrast, I am not, which is bonkers. I'm fifty-two, fairly successful, financially secure, confident and healthy with decent self-esteem, and I still see social media posts that make me feel like I am a bit shit.

Imagine how that feels if you are unemployed or on a zero-hours contract, insecure, with low self-esteem and with nobody in your life to make you laugh or share things with? It's not the fault of the people who post on social media. It's just the nature of the world we are living in today, where you are bombarded with messages that can depress you unless you have real-life friends to balance them out and show that Facebook, Instagram and Twitter don't give the full picture of anyone's life.

Our children have grown up in a different world from us. For mine, friendship is a multi-media experience. I remember going into my son Daniel's bedroom to tell him off for shouting at the video game he was playing, only to be told that he was talking to his mates, who were also playing the same game in their own bedrooms (while no doubt annoying their own parents). When I was growing up, playing with your mates meant you had to be in the same place. If you wanted to talk to them, you had to be in the same room, or at least sat on the stairs talking to them on the house phone.

Now, there are so many ways that you can send a message to a whole group of people who can then quickly engage with you in return. The difficulty with this is that, as we know, some of that engagement on social media can be negative. As well as the people you actually want in your life, it also allows those that you don't want to be in touch with to enter your world, in a way that never happened in the past.

I have experienced this negative side of social media myself. It's an odd feeling when I post a picture of myself walking my dog, with a humorous caption like 'I am not sure who is walking who', to be greeted in return by somebody posting: *'Fuck off, you're a shit comedian and I hope your dog gets run over!'*

I mean, *what* is going on in someone's head that makes them think that sending that message is worth their time? Plenty of people think that I am a shit comedian, but I don't think most of them are so angry about this that they decide to follow me on social media to share their opinion with me. I am also fairly certain their dislike of my perceived lack of comedic skills does not extend to them wanting my dog dead.

It is that kind of post that has made me use social media less. Firstly, I am not that sure enough people in the world want to know what I am doing on a daily basis to miss me telling them. Secondly, and more to the point, I can't be bothered with the one-in-a-thousand negative replies that I get. It used to bother Melanie a lot more than it ever did me, so much so that she deleted her Twitter account at my request. I felt it was better all round that Melanie did not have the opportunity, every day, to tell me, 'Look, I have found someone else who thinks you're a dickhead!'

I use Instagram most because there are much fewer negative responses and it's generally a more positive environment. I did some live streaming shows for Facebook, who also own Instagram, and had a social media meeting with them which was fascinating. They told me about the algorithms which can be used to increase your number of followers. Posting at certain times increases the number of people who look and follow you, as does the day and, especially, the content. It is in part because of that reason that certain celebrities are so active, because this builds their number of followers and, by extension, their 'influencer' status.

For example, there is also a huge correlation between celebrities posting videos of themselves in the gym exercising and the number of followers that they have. Apparently, if you post videos of yourself doing exercise, more people will follow you. I cannot imagine a better example of the difference between virtual and real friends than this. If I asked any of my mates to come and watch me exercise in a gym, I am 100 per cent certain they would all tell me to piss off – even if they were in the gym with me. It's just not the relationship we have.

Just try to imagine saying to a real person, 'Do me a favour – stand there for a few minutes and watch me sweat for a bit, and at the end I will come right up to your face and say something like, "Hashtag smashed it! Hashtag gotta want it more! Hashtag if it ain't hurtin' it ain't workin'!"' Nobody in their right mind is going to say, 'Yes please, thank you for asking me!' But send that out on social media and for some reason people like it and it's not weird.

Some celebrities have gained followers by asking someone else to film them while they lift weights in the gym and then sharing it on social media. *Nobody* could have seen that coming. I am not talking about celebrities who have a reason, such as they have a fitness video out, or are professional athletes who are demonstrating training techniques. I am talking about celebrities, from film stars to gameshow hosts, just doing exercises and trying as hard as they can to look as good as they can while someone films them doing it.

Going to the gym on social media may well increase your followers but it's not an avenue I want to go down. Firstly, I am not so proud of my performance in the gym that I want to brag about it. Secondly, I can't imagine who wants to watch such content. I can't get out of my head the mental image of some fat bloke in Northampton, sat in his underpants and vest eating chips in his kitchen as he watches a soap-opera star doing pull ups. I am fairly certain if this bloke turned up in the gym in person and asked any of these social media-sensations, 'Can I watch you sweat while I eat my chips in my underwear?' they would be horrified.

Mine was probably the last generation to know the difference between genuine sustainable friendships, and people who are talking because they are active in the same online group during their coffee break at work. I am not being a Luddite and suggesting that the internet's enhanced communication is a bad thing, but I admit that I operate on the basis that if somebody that I used to know fifteen years ago sends me a message and wants to be in touch, I tend to figure that, unless they were kidnapped or lost in the jungle for those fifteen years, the reason we have not been in touch is probably because we are not really friends. Trying to rekindle such relationships feels too much like hard work, given the effort I have to put in to maintaining the relationships I already have.

I do find WhatsApp useful. I like how it allows you to set up groups and keep in touch with them by texting the whole group. I have quite a few WhatsApp groups. Some are for very specific things. I have one with my brother and two sisters called Mum and Dad to discuss family matters that might pertain to our parents. Another group, Bishopx5, is for me, Melanie, Joe, Luke and Daniel to talk about our family matters.

These groups are great for communicating about essential family business but, of course, the problem with WhatsApp is that you find yourself in various splinter groups. You end up talking to the same people on different topics in different groups to the extent it gets confusing what you are talking about and you have to keep checking who else is in the splinter group in case you accidentally start slagging them off for their role in the larger group.

WhatsApp, Lads?

I also have a WhatsApp group called LADS. This features fifteen mates, all of whom I have known for more than twenty-five years and who nearly all date from my university days. I also belong to other splinter groups that contain different permutations of members of the main LADS group, which is why I know you have to be careful who you slag off.

LADS is by far the most active of all the WhatsApp groups on my phone. This is because it allows fifteen middle-aged men to take the piss out of each other 24/7. The only things that take the place of knocking each other are pictures of what people are drinking on holiday, comments about football matches as they are being played and weekly outbursts during *Question Time*. Mostly it is filled with jokes and sarcastic comments.

That, of course, is the defining feature of male friendships. All of the female friendships I have seen have always had the underlying urge to take care of each other. In male friendships, you know you are accepted when the rest of the group spend their time and energy trying to find the best ways to wind you up and take the piss.

The best way to illustrate this is to look at the difference between a hen party and a stag do. On a hen party, all of the girls will make sure their hen is looked after all night. She will be given a wedding veil to wear on her head and an L-plate to wear on her back, along with some wings and an inflatable penis to carry around so that she looks like a randy fairy. At some point in the evening she will be in the toilet with three of her best friends looking after her and holding her hair back as she pukes down the bog while crying, 'He's a bastard, but I love him!' One thing is certain: she will definitely get home safely because her friends will make sure she does.

By stark contrast, on a stag do there is always that moment in the bar at the start of the evening when you look around you and have a sense of what it must have felt like to go over the top of the trenches in World War I. You look around and you just know that not everyone there is going to make it. The evening may well begin with everybody toasting the stag and making a fuss of him but the time of the night will come when it is every man for himself, and the stag is left handcuffed to a lamppost somewhere in a strange city, on a street that nobody can remember and everyone will have forgotten who had the keys anyway. If he makes it home, he's done well. If he makes it to the wedding, it's a bonus.

Jane Fonda once said that women's friendships are 'like a renewable source of power'. I reckon male friendships are more like seatbelts in a car. You don't realise how important they are until something goes wrong and they are not there. That's how I feel about my LADS group. Many of them have worked much harder than I have to maintain our friendships and keep me involved, and I have valued their efforts more than they know or I would ever tell. In fact, over the last twenty-five to thirty years, there have been plenty of occasions where I have started to think I had less in common with the LADS group than I used to have. Then someone will call me and invite me to the pub and, just like Al Pacino says in *The Godfather Part III*: 'Just when I thought I was out ... they pull me back in.'

I have other, individual friends to whom I have been close over the same period. Such as my mate Jimmy, whom I played football with when I was sixteen and who has been around ever since and will I know always be there. Julie is the first person I spoke to on my first day at university, and we have remained close ever since. Then there's John, whom I have known since I was twelve: he worked on the first house that Melanie and I lived in and he's working on our new house twenty-seven years later.

However, as a group these LADS mates are the ones that I have spent the most time with over the last thirty years. There is no denying that there is a strong bond between us built on that shared history, and we are growing older together. You can always tell how close an old group of friends is when you see them ordering in a restaurant. With us, we have shared many things in the past, so when it comes to ordering from the menu and only one of us has brought a pair of glasses, they get passed around like some kind of ophthalmic joint.

It would be great to say that, as a group, we bonded through playing in the same sports teams, or through our love of hill-walking and outdoor pursuits, or through a book club. But the truth is that we bonded by all studying in Manchester at the same time and going to the same pubs. Over the years, we have tried cycling together and the odd game of football or golf, but ultimately it has always ended up in a pub. Nowadays we cut out all of the other stuff and just go straight to the bar.

We have been through weddings, funerals, divorces, the birth of children, football matches in European cities, stag weekends away and stag nights at home (sometimes when there was no one actually getting married), weekends away in UK cities and foreign countries for no reason other than to let off steam together, thirtieths, fourtieths, fiftieths, gigs, confidences shared, financial successes and crises, health scares, relocations, arguments, fall outs and dozens of reasons to not remain in touch. Yet somehow we have reached our fifties and are still all there, in the LADS WhatsApp group. I suspect the only reason anyone will leave it now is if they die – considering how we have lived at times, I'm surprised that hasn't happened to any of us yet.

One of my very favourite times with the LADS was the night that I revealed to them that I had started doing stand-up comedy. We were all out for the night. One of them had just become a dad and we were wetting the baby's head. Somebody (and no, it wasn't me) suggested that we go to a comedy club for a change and it happened to be the Frog and Bucket in Manchester, where, unknown to my mates, I had been quietly gigging for the last six months. When we all arrived, I slipped off and asked the manager if I could do a short set at some point. He agreed. So halfway through the show, while my friends thought I was in the toilet, to their utter amazement I was suddenly announced and appeared on the stage.

Once they got over their shock it went pretty well, but I have to say that from that point on, none of them have really accepted that I am a professional comedian. None of them think I am the funni-est bloke in our group, and I think they are right. Being funny with your friends is completely different from being funny on stage – and that is something that my mates didn't quite understand when I first started off. They were supportive and kept coming to see me, but it took a few gigs for them to realise that stand-up comedy is a different skill from mates' banter. This led to a rather unfortunate incident during my first run at the Edinburgh Festival in 2003.

Five of the LADS came to see my one-man show in a venue called the Cellar in the Pleasance Courtyard. It held about forty people. On this particular night, seventeen people had shown up, including my five mates. To be honest, for an unknown comic in Edinburgh this is not a bad audience, yet although I knew my mates were keen for me to impress, I also knew that they were disappointed for me when they walked down the stairs to find themselves in a tiny room that for the rest of the year was a cupboard. None of us had any other friends in showbusiness and none of us had ever been to the Edinburgh Festival before so I couldn't blame them for expecting something different. They certainly hadn't expected to be confronted with a basement with more empty seats than people in it.

To fit in an audience of forty people, a number I never achieved, some had to sit on benches at the front, then there was a row of chairs behind them, and finally stools at the back. My mates perched on the stools and the other twelve people scattered themselves between the benches and chairs. To my eyes, it looked better than many of the other nights: for most of my month-long run I had been pulling an average of twelve people.

I didn't really have a show, as such. I just tried to elicit some humour from chatting with the audience. It was the third week of my run and by now I had learned the lesson that if you are going to try and entertain people for an hour, you need to have a structure and a plan – basically, you need to *have a show*. If I hadn't known this myself, the reviewers who came to see me had certainly helpfully pointed it out to me. I had been totally unprepared for how difficult a month at the Edinburgh Festival can be, and had my mates not already booked the train tickets and hotel for the weekend, I probably would have tried to persuade them not to come.

Yet they were determined to show their support for me – a little too determined, it turned out. There was no stage in the venue and on the night that they were there, I was simply stood in front of the rows of seats, as usual, chatting to the audience and trying to pull any nugget I could from them to create some comedy.

I was getting nowhere. As the festival attracts people from all over the world, I am not sure that everyone in the room understood English – or at least not my version of English. Even when I asked standard questions such as, 'What's your name, and where are you from?' I was being greeted by blank stares. Then one man in the second row told me, 'We have paid to listen to you, not for you to listen to us.'

I was about to reply with a friendly heckler putdown when a voice rang out – one of my friends on the stools at the back of the room: *'Oi, Dickhead, leave him alone! Eh, Bish! Tell them about when we went to Amsterdam on Duff's stag do, and you got locked in that nightclub toilet!'*

My mates started laughing among themselves and telling each other even better stories than the Amsterdam locked-in-the-toilet one. It was soon clear I had lost what little audience I had. Ten minutes before the end of the show, the people who weren't my mates all left, accompanied by my mates shouting after them: 'Where are you going? We've got *loads* of stories about him!' I stood, watched the room emptying and wondered how I was friends with such well-meaning saboteurs.

Afterwards, I patiently explained to the lads that it didn't really help me to heckle with stories that nobody else in the room would know anything about. For comedy to work, you experience something, you recognise something in it that is funny, and you share what you recognise with an audience. If the other people recognise the same thing as you, then everyone in the room will spontaneously laugh. Talking about a stag do that nobody in the audience went to, and using it as a basis for comedy, has some obvious flaws. The moral of the tale is that when anecdotes end with 'You had to be there!', for it to be funny, you probably had to be there.

My mates were full of apologies and, to be fair to them, they took it on board. The next time members of the LADS fraternity came to my one-man show, everyone agreed in advance not to heckle. This was at the Leicester Square Theatre in central London. It is a great 400-seat room, but it also has a small studio room that can hold around 35 people. I played this small room in 2008 after another Edinburgh run which had been just as unsuccessful as the previous ones. Despite this, my agent saw the opportunity to get me some exposure via a one-man show in London.

This would not have been a bad strategy … had anybody actually come to see it. That night, I got an audience of eighteen people. To put that into context, with London having a population of around eight million people, I managed to get 0.000225 per cent of them to come and see me. Even that figure is too inflated, as half of the audience were my mates, and the other nine people were made up of two Japanese tourists (one who spoke English, and kept translating the punchlines to the other one), four people who had actually bought tickets, two friends of my agent and a member of the theatre staff.

This time my situation was different from when the lads had come to the Edinburgh Festival. The stakes were much higher for me because I had left my job to pursue comedy full-time. Rather than feeling embarrassed for me, my mates tried to lift me up by laughing slightly too much, and too loudly, because it was clear without their presence the night would have been a disaster.

They took me for a curry after the show. As we walked through Soho to the curry house (they insisted on paying, as it was obvious that I had not made any money that night) the LADS were all full of encouragement. We were in our forties and they had just watched their friend walk away from a good job to chase a dream. They had also just watched me stand in a half-empty room struggling to get people to laugh.

That night, I promised them that if I ever managed to get booked on something like *Live at the Apollo*, I would get them all tickets. The amazing thing is that it did happen – and only eighteen months later. I asked the producer if I could have guest tickets. He asked how many and he nearly choked on the phone when I said that I wanted twelve. He explained that the normal allocation is two. Somehow, he managed to get me the full amount and the lads can be seen in the audience on my first *Live at the Apollo* performance. This would have been a perfect night had I not got a phone call late that night from that same producer. He was fuming because two of the acts' cabs had been nicked by twelve mystery people who had arrived at the stage door needing a taxi, telling the young assistant producer that they were 'John Bishop's writers'.

My friends have since been to see me play arenas and we have all stood backstage remembering those early, empty gigs. Only one thing hasn't changed: my mates still don't think that I am the funniest in our group, and I still agree.

Doing It for the Kids

The reality is that as you grow older and change the way you live your life, so do the people around you. Anyone with children will know this. When you are a parent, there is a phase in your life when you do not pick your friends: they are simply selected from the parents of your children's friends.

There is no other significant decision in your life that you would allow a five-year-old to make, yet when you become a parent you find that having children in the same school gives you a common bond with people that you would previously have never imagined spending time with. Before you know it, you are arranging play dates for the kids, helping out together at the football, having barbecues, and then having dads' nights and even holidays together.

This is all OK when the kids are five or six. Buddying up with other parents helps with the crowd control. However, when you get to the business end of school and it comes to exams, or who gets into the school teams, those fellow parents become competitors who will gladly drop in how well their offspring is doing, and how hard they are working, when you can't even get your own sixteen-year-old to remember what day their exams are on.

The kids grow up and leave and you realise that you like their friends' parents less than you imagined you did, particularly when the kids don't even talk to each other anymore. Then you realise that your first impressions were right – you have nothing in common with them, and now you have to find a way to extricate yourself from the old 'School Run' WhatsApp group without anyone knowing.

This is all predicated on the assumption that these 'friends' like you, when in reality they are probably feeling exactly the same as you are. There should be an annual review in friendships like you have at work with the HR department. You can sit and have a review meeting, set objectives for the coming year ahead, do a SWOT analysis of your relationship and see if it still matches your joint objectives.*

There is a lot of truth in the cliché of grumpy old men retiring into sheds to fix models rather than talk to other people. I can easily find myself withdrawing. I use excuses like going for a long bike

---

* *Or, you can simply not reply to a few texts and hope they go away.*

ride alone rather than joining a club, or saying I have some work to do that requires me to be alone. In themselves these things are not negative activities, but I have learned over the years that when I withdraw, I am less happy than when I am with people. Scientific evidence backs this up and suggests that people who participate in team sports release up to seven times more endorphins that people who do sport individually. I think it goes beyond sport: *people need people*.

Now that I have been in showbusiness for over a decade, I have genuine friends from that world. It is an odd thing to make friends with famous people because it takes a little time to get over the fact that you are both famous. In a strange way, you have to un-learn what you thought you knew about each other because when someone is famous you already know something about them, and start seeing each other as ordinary people who live extraordinary lives. The bonus is you can talk about the extraordinary life you both have without coming across as a knob, as you would if you did the same thing while talking to your mates.

As you grow older, friendship grows more important than ever. It is essential that you have good friends and that you put the hours into keeping them. It may be easier said than done on occasions, but it's worth it. And my Google trawl for quotes on friendship threw up a great one from Ralph Waldo Emerson, a prominent figure in the mid-nineteenth century transcendental movement, which believed in the inherent goodness of people and nature: *The only way to have a friend is to be one*.

That makes sense to me.

5.

HOW TO STILL BE FUNNY

WHEN THE WORD 'DAD' is added to the description of an activity, it is rarely a positive addition. In fact, it generally implies that the dad is not very good at that activity.

Take 'dad dancing' and 'dad jokes'. 'Dad dancing' basically describes a set of rhythmic convulsions set to music with no real attempt to match the beat, because he will do the same dance no matter what is being played. It is a man whose body seems to have been fused at the pelvis, so that the legs work independently of the top half. The arms appear to be being controlled by someone else, while the head nods *almost* in time with the music. It is unclear if the man is using his head as a metronome or just trying to look cool as he tries to get everyone else to join in.

Dad jokes seems to exist in that space between something being funny in your head and becoming completely unfunny as it leaves your mouth. Most people have an internal filter that ensures that jokes like that are never told: dads don't. In fact, when dad jokes pop out, they appear to surprise the dad as much as the people that he tells them to. They are the verbal equivalent of the middle-aged fart – everyone in the room is left slightly embarrassed apart from the owner who can seem inappropriately proud.

Personally, I think the phenomenon of dad jokes has been blown out of proportion. *I don't think we are all that bad*. Television has not helped because middle-aged male characters in TV sitcoms simply aren't funny. Or rather, not when they're trying to be. They don't make jokes, they *are* the joke, always floundering around, out of touch, getting the wrong end of the stick, being pityingly tolerated by their families and the world in general. It's how we've always been portrayed, from *Till Death Us Do Part* to *George and Mildred*, *Terry and June* to *Outnumbered*. The message has always been that middle-aged men just aren't funny.

Clearly, as a middle-aged professional comedian, I have a vested interest in believing that you can still be funny as you get older. I plan my live tours a year in advance and when I have tour dates booked, I know I don't have the option to turn up and not be funny. I know that on any given date, at 8pm in some theatre somewhere in the UK next year, I have to be funny because there will be a roomful of people waiting for me to make them laugh.

As I have explained earlier, at this point I don't have the first idea what I will say when I go on those tour dates. I don't know if I will be funny but I do know that *I've got to be*. It puts pressure on you. Ask any comedian – having to think about that does induce a certain constant low-level anxiety. I think for most comedians, however, that is what drives them on: the sense that they will have to say something, and though they don't even know what it is yet, it will make people laugh. That's a great feeling.

The Best Medicine

In terms of growing old, being funny and enjoying your life, laughing as you age is essential. It helps to keep you young and also helps deal with the stresses of life. The Mayo Clinic, out in Phoenix, Arizona in America, is one of the leading medical institutions in the world, and promotes laughter on its website in order for its patients to reduce their physical and mental stress. I first came across the Mayo Clinic when I was working in the pharmaceutical industry, where clinical trials used to prove the efficacy and safety of a drug have enhanced credibility if they come from an institution that is held in high esteem. The Mayo Clinic was, and is, one of the best.

Years ago, when we were struggling to find a clear diagnosis for my son Joe's auto-immune condition, I took him for a week at the Mayo Clinic. Joe underwent a series of tests and we met a variety of top clinicians, all of whom had elements of the titular character that Hugh Laurie played in the US TV medical drama *House*. I don't mean they all walked with a cane and were socially awkward. It was more than they kept trying to see the problem from a different angle.

I understand that I only had the top-of-the-range option of the Mayo Clinic because I could pay for it and, like any parent, it was a simple decision for me. If I could not make Joe's medical condition go away, I would give anything to anyone who could. Yet in the end, the Mayo team concluded that the diagnosis reached by Dr Phil Riley and his team at the Royal Manchester Children's Hospital was correct: Joe had Cogan's Syndrome, a condition that manifests itself by affecting the sight and/or the hearing of the sufferer.

This diagnosis was on one level reassuring and on another devastating. It meant that Joe's current course of treatment was correct, but so was the future prognosis. There was no magic bullet pill that would correct what was wrong with Joe, and we would have to continue to fight to retain as much of his hearing as we could. We would also have to continue to pray that his eyesight remained unaffected.

We continue to do so. Joe's battle will be lifelong and there may never be a time when he will be off medication or away from the threat of a flare up that may cause further irreparable damage. Having this sword of Damocles over your head as a teenage boy can't have been easy and I have perhaps not always cut him the slack he deserved because of it. As a young man it has made him stronger, but if I could swap places with him, I would do so in a heartbeat.

Not least because it would make me a handsome twenty-five-year-old man, with a world of potential ahead of me.

Writing this book, I turned to the Mayo Clinic again in happier circumstances when I was researching the effects of laughter on your wellbeing. Their website explains that laughter enhances your intake of oxygen-rich air, which stimulates your heart, lungs and muscles, and increases the endorphins that are released by your brain. Laughing also empties your lungs of more air than you take in, which has a cleansing effect as it positively affects the way that blood flows around the body, reducing the likelihood of heart disease. Because a good laugh is spontaneous, it fires up and then cools down your stress response, increases then decreases your heart rate and blood pressure, resulting in a relaxed feeling.

Researchers say that fifteen minutes of laughter a day is as important for your heart as thirty minutes of exercise three times a week.

But laughter isn't just a quick pick-me-up. It's also good for you over the long term and may well improve your immune system. Negative thoughts manifest into chemical reactions that can affect your body by bringing more stress into your system and decreasing your immunity. By contrast, positive thoughts can release neuropeptides that help fight stress and potentially more-serious illnesses.

Regardless of what is making you laugh, the act of laughing makes you feel better. Laughter has been shown to be such a powerful healer of the body that it may even ease pain by causing the body to produce its own natural painkillers. I am not suggesting that your dentist gives you a tickle rather than a local anaesthetic before he yanks your molar out, but you get my drift.

It's a physical and psychological impossibility to laugh and be depressed at the same time. They are opposite poles and it's only possible for the body to do one or the other, meaning that laughing is the fastest way to lift your mood. So, when people – of any age – are feeling down, they will probably benefit from seeing a good comedy or meeting up with friends who make them laugh. It may sound a bit daft to tell someone who is depressed that they should sit down and watch *Only Fools and Horses** or go to a comedy club with their mates, but it has been clinically proven to work.

Laughing is a key ingredient in enhancing wellbeing and, as research has suggested that longevity is 70 per cent determined

---

* *This does not just apply to* Only Fools and Horses. *Other sitcoms are available, but David Jason falling through the bar never gets old.*

by environment and lifestyle choices, choosing to laugh on a daily basis is something that should no longer be regarded as a bonus but instead should be a part of what we strive to do daily, especially as we get older. Dads are simply trying to extend their life and that of their family by telling crap jokes.

This growing recognition of the benefits of laughing has even led to thousands of people around the world attending Laughter Yoga classes. Laughter Yoga was created by Dr Madan Kataria, a medic in India who was interested in the body's response to laughter, even if that laughter was 'fake' and was not being stimulated by something external like a joke. He started in a park in Mumbai in 1995 with just five participants, and now there are thousands of Laughter Clubs in more than a hundred countries around the world.

What Laughter Yoga proponents suggest is that as long as you are willing to laugh, you will get the psychological and physiological benefits of 'genuine' laughter because your body does not know you have not been told a joke. It also seems apparent that fake laughter soon turns into 'real' laughter, further enhancing the benefits received. I am now reassured that even if I think someone in the audience at one of my gigs is only pretending to laugh, at least it is still doing them some good.

Despite all the evidence that laughter is good for your health and will keep you going longer, it is fair to assume that older people will want to be made to laugh by someone who is the same as them, i.e. another old person. They don't want to be eighty years old and sat in a wheelchair while some kid with spiky hair tells them their funniest Snapchat story and takes the piss out of the contestants on *Love Island*. The danger of the dad joke falling on its arse because the people who hear it don't understand it is greatly reduced if the dad is surrounded by like-minded, age-appropriate people: basically, an audience of dads.*

I think comedians all worry that they might get less funny as they grow older. Thankfully, so far I haven't personally found this to be the case. I think my last tour was the best that I have ever done. As I said, I had all this new, very rich material about me turning fifty and my kids leaving home. It was still very universal stuff that people who are growing older, and especially people of my age, can relate to.

I think that the trick is to accept, in comedy as in life, that you change as you grow older, and some of the things that you find funny aren't as obvious as before. It's amazing how quickly I have found myself going from developing material about going to the gym or running a marathon to talking about being in a doctor's having a prostrate examination. My comedy goes where my life takes it.

One thing that has never changed over the years, and throughout my entire career, is that my kids don't find me funny. Not off stage, anyway. They have been to see shows I have done, and some of them have even worked on my tours and television shows. They think my material is OK and that I am basically all right at what I do, but when we are at home, it's completely different.

When we are at home, I'm just 'Dad'. That's fair enough. It would be a bit weird if I were walking around the house and my lads were going, 'Oh great, here comes Bish, he's a good laugh!' They don't do that, and now they are totally blasé about what I

Having said this, research suggests that, on average, women laugh 125 per cent more than men. I can guarantee that if I am ever on a stage and there is someone in the audience with a brilliant laugh, nine times out of ten it will be a woman. So I don't just want an audience of dads, thanks.

do. When they were little and I was starting out, they used to be excited if I was on television. Now, they don't bother to watch me half of the time, and that's fine with me. Not many children watch their parents working.

I did have a glimmer of hope recently. *GQ* magazine was running a feature about Father and Son Day, a charity initiative which benefits the Royal Marsden Hospital and gets men talking activity about health, particularly male cancer. The magazine asked me if I would do an interview and photo shoot. It wasn't clear to me from the request that I got whether they wanted me and my dad or me and my sons, so I proposed both and the magazine went with it.

It was a great day. When else does any family get the opportunity to have their hair and clothes styled and get photographed by a top professional magazine photographer? My dad came down to London on the train with my mum and at the end of the shoot, I asked the photographer to sit my mum in the picture too so we would have something unique to put up at home. The pictures were brilliant. My lads all looked smart and it was gratifying to see that at least the generations of my family have one thing in common, because my dad, my sons and I all asked the stylist if we could keep the clothes, or at least buy them at a discount. There is something in our genes that makes us all want a bargain.

It was also great to see my dad in make-up. My dad is in his seventies and has swallows tattooed on the back of his hands: that tells you everything you need to know, I think, about the world he grew up in. To see my dad having a make-up artist apply some powder to his face showed me just how far my family's life has changed from what was predetermined for us by our background.

After the photographs we all did a video chat for the website. The journalist inevitably asked me who I thought was the funniest person in our family and I said 'My dad' – not purely out of a sense of duty but because he is. He has a sharp, dry sense of humour that I have always enjoyed. My answer received 'Isn't that nice?' nods of approval from everyone there, and then the interviewer asked Joe, Luke and Daniel the big question: 'Do you find your dad funny?'

The question seemed to hang in the air. None of them wanted to commit. It was like that moment when someone presents you with an ugly baby and you just don't know what to say. If you say, 'Oh, it's beautiful!' then you risk upsetting them because they will know you are a liar – but at the same time, you can't really say, 'Wow, what a pig-ugly baby that is!' Because there is always the danger they may not realise it themselves.

My boys just said, 'Er, yeah,' which made it worse. I could have handled a straight 'No', but not an apologetic 'Er, yeah.' That sounded as if it was being extracted under duress, like in a hostage video. I knew that *GQ*'s readers would look at that clip and immediately think, *OK, they don't think their dad is funny.*

I used to wish that my boys found me funny. Now, it is a battle that I no longer fight because I have realised that they are not my target audience. If I was basing my career upon being funny to three men, aged between twenty-one and twenty-five, who happen to look a lot like me, then I would have very limited appeal. I also won't be able to pay the bills as I don't see any of them ever buying a ticket. So I have decided that, as a professional who on a good day can sell well in most venues, my sons' judgement is not the one that matters to me. I have reverted to the safe haven of all comedians who don't go down as well as they would have liked and blame the crowd. *'Look, lads,'* I have told the boys. *'I'm a professional comedian and communicator! I can say the things I'm saying to you now on stage, to an audience, and those people are going to laugh. So, if you don't laugh, it's your fault for being a shit audience.'*

To be funny, you need to find your audience. And that's why I think that dad jokes are just jokes told to the wrong people.

Humour Ages Well

Getting older is definitely not a limiting factor when it comes to stand-up comedy. You just have to keep going. The American comedian George Burns was often described as 'the oldest comedian on earth' and was performing well into his nineties. He signed a lifetime contract at Caesars Palace in Las Vegas when he was ninety-six. He even had London Palladium booked to perform in after his hundredth birthday but sadly passed away, aged one hundred, after a career of nearly ninety years. He smoked ten to fifteen cigars and drank three or four vodka martinis every day. I once saw a journalist ask him what his doctor thought of his lifestyle. Quick as a flash, George said, 'Nothing, he's dead!'

Joan Rivers was eighty-one when she died. Her last performance had come a month earlier at the eighty-seater Laurie Beechman Theatre in Manhattan, during a new material night. *A new material night.* Just think about that for a minute. Joan Rivers was on stage, aged eighty-one, with notes and new jokes that she was trying out in a small theatre the night before she had her fatal heart attack.

What kind of octogenarian woman wants to think of funny things to say, write them down, get dressed, drag herself out of the house and stand in front of a room of strangers trying to make them laugh? It is the very essence of being a stand-up comedian because nobody in their right mind would do it. Just imagine comedy clubs all over the country with their open mic nights full of grannies, getting up and doing new material about the funny staff from their care home or what the world was like before television. Joan Rivers showed that you can still be funny if you still keep trying to be funny.

The best example of a comedian who wanted to keep going that I have met was Ken Dodd. Ken had developed a reputation over the years for doing shows that would go on for four or five hours. Even throwing in the odd song and some old material, that is an incredible amount of time to be talking for anyone, let alone a man who was still doing gigs months before his death at the age of ninety. To do that you have to really want to do it, and you have to love it.

I had the pleasure of meeting Ken Dodd on a couple of occasions. One was after seeing him perform at the London Palladium in 2007. It was fantastic to watch a real craftsman. He had great presence and great stagecraft which you do not always notice unless someone doesn't have it. Ken made it look easy. After a career spanning seven decades, he had spent a lifetime on stage, so it looked a natural home for him.

I was invited to say hello to him after the Palladium show. Considering that he was eighty years of age at this point and had just done a three-hour stand-up show, I expected to be led in to meet someone who would not remember who I was, and to be shuffled out as quickly as possible. However, when I was taken to the private bar upstairs where the guests were having drinks, Ken came straight over as soon as he saw me. We shook hands and I was busy complimenting him on his show when he said, 'Yes, John. Yes, very good. Thank you for coming. Now, listen. Credit crunch. It's all over the news, this new phrase: credit crunch. Have you got anything on it?'

I didn't know what to say. I was not expecting a conversation with a comedic national treasure to turn into a discussion about the financial turmoil across the globe, one caused by the sudden reduction in loans due to the tightening of credit facilities, thus resulting in less liquidity as money became less available.

'Er, I only know what I've seen on the news, Ken,' I told him. 'It seems that it's going to be harder to get a loan and that will obviously affect the housing market if people can't get mortgages ...'

Ken Dodd looked at me like I was mad. 'I know *that*, John, but do you have a gag about it?' he asked. 'There has to be something funny about it! Maybe, "Is a credit crunch a chocolate bar that you eat now and pay for next week?" What do you think?'

I couldn't believe it. Ken was eighty, had just done a three-hour show and received a standing ovation at one of the most famous theatre venues in the world. And now he was already looking for new material. It's a bit like sporting champions: they never dwell on what they have just done, they are already looking ahead. Ken Dodd was the Mo Farah of comedy and was already in training for his next marathon.

That is what you need to be doing to still be funny. Just keep looking for things to be funny about. Keep trying new things and keep looking outside of yourself because, as anyone who is heading into middle age will tell you, your body quickly becomes your least favourite subject matter. You have to talk about what's happening in the wider world because, if you don't, you find yourself talking about your knees hurting. Not only is this a depressing reminder for both you and the audience about your physical decline, but it also quickly runs out of steam in terms of humour. I don't want to be on stage saying, 'Come on, give yourselves a round of applause, at least we all managed to get here. Not sure how many of us will make it home, but at least we got here.' I don't want to be doing a tour for old people called *Every Show Is a Bonus*.

When you're doing observational comedy, as I am, you can't escape the fact that it is all about what you observe – and the main thing that you observe, every day, is yourself. But what if your life is becoming less comedic and edgy? What if the things you are observing are nice city breaks, walking around looking at museums, or a river cruise down the Danube, as recommended by Jane McDonald? I think the trick is just to be honest about it all, and about yourself, and hopefully it will still hit home (as long as you throw the odd knob gag in).

Having said that, sometimes you can offend people without ever expecting to do so. On my last tour, I did a bit about nut allergies. *'We must have the weakest human beings alive ever,'* I said, *'because kids today are allergic to everything. I had never heard of nut allergies when I was at school, so when did it became fashionable? Where were all the kids with nut allergies then? They probably never even made it to school. They must have had a Marathon bar on the way in and never made it. Oh – and if you are under twenty-five, that's a Snickers.'*

I told that joke on the tour as it's a bit of an observation about nut allergies because I genuinely do not recall anyone having one when I was at school. It's also a joke about Marathons now being called Snickers, which is a bit nostalgic for people of my age. It's not the greatest joke ever and it was not even a main joke in the show, just something that I would chuck in now and again. Then, one night, I was at Nottingham Arena, a venue that holds 8,000 people, and when I did my nut-allergy material, a man at the back stood up and screamed something at me.

Normally, in a comedy environment, you can hear a heckle from the back and respond to it. In an arena it's not so easy. I was also more apprehensive than usual because I was in Nottingham. The last time I was touring in Nottingham and somebody in the audience shouted, it was because a fight had broken out. I had thought that something was wrong because my jokes were not getting the same response as usual, and then I noticed that the audience all seemed to be looking to one side of the arena.

'John, there's a fight, mate!' somebody shouted and I then realised that everybody was looking in the direction of the fracas. It was obviously quite a serious incident so I asked the cameraman to pick it up on his camera so that the venue security could locate the culprits. This proved to be a big mistake, as the fight then appeared on the big screen behind me, meaning that the audience started watching it, taking sides and shouting encouragement. I had no option but to sit on my stool and commentate on the fight while the police and the security broke up what I was later found out was two families brawling. As police and security were dragging the biggest of the brawlers away – and it took four of them to do it – the bloke broke free and ran towards the stage. 'Bish, fucking great show, mate!' he yelled before they jumped on him again and dragged him out. I guess that was a good review.

This previous rowdy experience in Nottingham meant that, when I heard a shout from the back this time around, I felt I had no option but to pause and to ask the man in question to repeat himself.

'You twat!' He shouted again. 'My son has a nut allergy!'

There was a murmur in the crowd, I had paused the gig so everyone had heard what the guy had said. Some people were telling him to be quiet and some were waiting to see what I would say back.

In the past, in a comedy-club environment, I might have said something crude, like 'Mate, if *you* haven't got a nut allergy, I would suggest that you buy all of your mates a Snickers bar each and find out who his dad is!' However, this was an arena and as I head into middle age, I have hopefully grown not just older but also wiser. *'Mate,'* I said, *'you have got it wrong. I am not taking the piss out of your son or anyone with a nut allergy. I am just stating a fact that nut allergies never used to exist, so it's not a joke about allergies – it's a question about the epidemiology of nut allergies and how the world is changing.'*

Now, this was not the standard heckle put-down but it got a cheer from the crowd. However, it did not appease the man, and as he walked out of the arena in protest, he looked back at me and yelled, 'You can still fuck off!'

I think that was probably one of the best heckler put-downs I have ever come out with. The great thing was that a journalist from *The Times* was there to review the show. He very kindly gave me a four-star review, but I was far more pleased that his review contained my put-down and thus the word 'epidemiology'. I think I can safely say that in the entire history of comedy, that word has never before appeared in a comedy review, and I doubt it will ever happen again.

This is the great change in how I see my comedy as I get older. I want it to still remain funny, but I also want it to be factually correct.

6.
HOW TO GO ON HOLIDAY

THERE CAN'T BE MANY parts of modern life that have changed more in my lifetime than the way we take our holidays. Back in the day, come August, Brits traditionally headed off to Blackpool, Clacton-on-Sea or Bognor Regis. It wasn't until the 1960s and 1970s that package tours were born and families started jetting to the Costa Brava. Nowadays, British people make seventy-two million journeys a year abroad, for business or pleasure. Back in the 1970s, it was still only the well-heeled and well-off families that got on a plane.

My family was not one of them. When I was a kid, flying abroad for a holiday seemed about as likely as flying to the moon. It just wasn't something that even occurred to us. We went camping, we went to Pontins holiday camp a couple of times, and we went to Bala in North Wales. That doesn't mean we didn't enjoy the holidays: they were great. I used to love going to Wales, because I could pretend that I was abroad because all the Welsh road signs didn't make any sense to me.

As I grew older, and had left home, I still didn't really go on traditional holidays as such. I went to Benidorm or Majorca with football teams and I coached football in America for three years on the bounce, which meant that I got to travel all over the States. I had a few mad ones in Majorca, but I didn't really have the usual sun, sea and sand two-week breaks: I was just busy doing other stuff.

The first big change in my holiday regime came when I met Melanie and we got married. Our lives were such a mad rush in those days that the first holiday that Melanie and I had together as a couple was our honeymoon. It was daft, really. We had been away with other people before, but the first holiday with just the two of us together was our honeymoon in Kenya.

If I have a lesson for anybody, it is this: *Go on holiday with somebody before you marry them*. It's not that our honeymoon was a bad thing or that Melanie and I discovered terrible things about each other. It wasn't like that. It was more that it would have been nice for us to have had three or four years before children arrived doing fun stuff together because some things are harder to do with children in tow, like basically everything.

Our first son, Joe, was born fourteen months after we were married. And that's when everything changes: when the kids come along. That is when you first think about organising these things called family holidays. The first challenge was booking them. There was no internet booking in those days. I would say to Melanie, 'Look, this is what we can afford this year,' and we'd spend ages looking at the holiday pages on Teletext* or she would go down

---

* *Teletext – where the graphics always looked like robot porn.*

the travel agent and phone me from there and tell me what they had. I can only say: thank God the internet got invented.

When we first got married, Melanie's mum lived in France and so we used to drive the kids on holiday to the Dordogne to stay with her. They were good holidays, but I remember a lot of stress. Part of it was my fault. I used to do this ridiculous thing where I viewed any upcoming holidays as a deadline that I had to get all of my work finished by, so I'd be up until all hours of the morning for days just before we went away. It meant that the first few days of the holiday, I would always be completely knackered.

The reality of any holiday for married couples is that you spend the first few days having all the arguments you haven't had time to have in the previous six months. A long drive to France is the perfect time to do that. In 2016, a study by the University of Washington found that filings for divorce in America peaked after Christmas and in August, after the summer holidays. *'Often, couples find that being in a hotel for two weeks with someone can irritate you,'* the report noted. *'You can't escape to work and the enforced closeness can highlight all the things you don't like about your partner, rather than the other way around.'* You can say that again.

The other big factor for Melanie and me, of course, was that we had had our boys very quickly and very close together, which meant that we had three young lads to deal with. We had no real choice but for me to buy my first people carrier, and I was very conscious that a people carrier is the motor vehicle equivalent of wearing corduroy slacks. It's like you are saying to the rest of the world, 'Look, I've just given up now! *This* is all I want from life! I am comfortable so please don't judge me.' But for a few years, it was a necessity for us.

An argumentative journey with three very young kids in a people carrier from the North of England to the Dordogne can last a very, very long time. That was how it felt, anyway. This was way before the digital age had dawned so there were no iPads to plug the kids into. Apart from asking 'Are we nearly there yet?' every two minutes, the only things that kept the kids amused was when they were throwing things at me while I was driving or the youngest two were filling their nappies.

You can only go to the Dordogne so many times and as the kids got older, we started taking them on all-inclusive package holidays. Before the advent of budget airlines led more holidaymakers to do their own thing, package holidays ruled the roost in Britain in the 1990s. We did some great ones – to Turkey and Greece and Spain and Portugal – but we also had to accept that all-inclusive package holidays come with their own particular challenges.

They would start at the airport. We'd get on the plane and I would sit and look around the aircraft and just *know* that we had picked the wrong package. It's never a good sign when a family turn up and they are all wearing the same football kit. No matter how liberal you think you are, a holiday is a precious thing and you don't want to share it with other people who are potentially going to ruin your holiday by simply having theirs. *For God's sake,* you think, *I hope they're not staying at our hotel.* But, yes, *they are.* You get put on a coach to the same hotel, get given the same wristbands, and the football family spend the next week viewing the all-you-can-eat-buffet as a personal challenge. They are on a mission to clear the whole table and get their money's worth.

We did some great holidays with our kids. We did the Valley of the Kings in Egypt and we did adventure holidays with loads of stuff for them to do ... but then they hit the teenage years and they just don't want to go with you. They started wanting to stay behind at home instead. We would have all of these arguments where we'd have a fourteen-year-old boy who could not begin to understand why we wouldn't leave him in the house for two weeks on his own. *'What's wrong with you?'* he'd ask us. *'Don't you trust me?'*

When they were teenagers, we never left the boys behind when we went on holiday, but we had the odd night when we would leave them on their own. Melanie's mum had by then moved from the Dordogne to a cottage three doors from us, so we knew she could keep an eye on them. Once, when he was about seventeen, we left Daniel, our youngest, on his own. Like a dickhead, he forgot that his grandma lived three doors from us and threw a big party. He remembered when his gran turned up in her nightie at the house at 4am and sent all of his mates home. For some reason, he assumed she wouldn't tell us about it. He was wrong. Eileen was a great spy.

Now the lads have all grown up and left home, it's nearly impossible to do a family holiday. Our last one was a couple of years ago when we all went to Sweden for New Year's Eve. It was great, but Melanie and I have to *buy* their time now. It's a life lesson: if you want your kids in their twenties to go on holiday with you, it has really got to be a bloody good holiday, or why would they bother?

We never went as a family to the big British holiday destination of the last twenty years – Ibiza. In fact, I didn't go to Ibiza until I was thirty-five and I was on a stag weekend. In all honesty, I felt like I was a losing contestant standing next to Jim Bowen on *Bullseye* as he said, 'Come and have a look what you could have won!' What had I missed out on? I stood in one of the clubs, looked around me and thought, *If only I had been here ten years ago. I would have looked fabulous!* Beautiful, svelte people in clothes that

127

ranged from glitter-covered bikinis and stilettos to white Giorgio Armani suits moved around as if on wheels. It was clear that they were part of the ecosystem of Ibiza nightclub life. Then I noticed the rest of us – those of us that were the wallpaper of the venue. We were there but you don't notice us because you were so dazzled by those who *belong*.

We were those ones who sweat, who have loaded up with drinks before entering to save money, who the barman never sees, and who never see what the world looks like from the VIP area. We were the nearly dressed, wearing the kind of Armani clothes you find in TK Maxx: the right brand but the wrong size that you buy anyway because you will never own anything that looks so cool, even though it would only look cool on someone else.

I did get in the Ibiza club VIP area a few years later, thanks to some friends who had done well for themselves. It was like being given a brand new pair of football boots and told to go and train with Liverpool: pretty quickly, it's apparent you don't belong there. When the only reason that you have got past the magic VIP rope is because someone has paid enough money for it to happen, then you know you are only a pretender. You are not one of the beautiful people or the really cool people. You are the mate of someone who got you in, and even the rope you are sat behind knows you are on the wrong side of it.

City Breaks

Now I'm in my fifties and the kids have moved out, it's just Melanie and me going on holiday. In the past, we used to want quite different things from our breaks and it was a bit of a source of tension. She has always seen a holiday as a rest, whereas I have viewed it as an excuse to go somewhere different and try something new. My ideal holiday used to be, 'Let's do two days in one place, then move on!' I liked it to be non-stop and all-action.

Middle age knocks that out of you. I don't have as much energy to do stuff and Melanie doesn't want to lie in the sun all the time anymore, so we have kind of met in the middle. We have started doing what a lot of middle-aged couples do and going on city breaks. City breaks are actually the most popular holidays for British people, or at least those of a certain age – the Association of British Travel Agents (ABTA) reckons 48 per cent of Brits went on one in 2018, even more than went on beach holidays.

Actually, Melanie and I used to do city breaks a few years ago, but they were bonkers. We'd fly to a strange city, stay in a hotel and have loads of cocktails and wild sex, and leave bleary-eyed the next morning. The city breaks we are doing nowadays are very different. Now we wear comfortable shoes, walk around with a map, get on a city tour bus, feel like we've learned something, and go home promising to read more of the guidebook and go back another time.

We have joined the ranks of the middle-aged couples who are attempting to enhance their sex lives by walking around European cities. Being a man, I will admit that there is always a deal being hatched in my head: *If a weekend in Dublin equates to a quickie before breakfast, then Dubrovnik has to be worth dressing up as a nurse?* I have probably revealed too much and Melanie will go mad if she reads this, because I have never told anyone I like dressing up as a nurse.

When you are middle-aged, you go on city breaks because they are exactly what it says on the tin – a break. Or if you want a proper middle-aged holiday, there is nothing more appropriate than a cruise. In 2017, nearly two million people from Britain and Ireland set sail on cruises – the highest figure ever. More than 700,000 of them went to the Mediterranean, with 450,000 sailing to the big growth area, Northern Europe, and 22,000 taking exploration cruises to places such as the Antarctic, Arctic and Galapagos Islands. A lot of British cruise holidaymakers are in their seventies – but, tellingly, the average age is now fifty-six.

Melanie always wanted to go on a cruise and I always thought that I couldn't think of anything worse. I hate the idea of containment and the thought of being trapped on a ship, unable to escape. The idea of being led around by a tour guide with a load of other mature people was anathema to me. But last year, Melanie finally convinced me to go on one. It was to the Caribbean – and it was linked in to Esther the Wonder Pig, a curly-tailed phenomenon that Melanie follows on Instagram.

For those of you lucky enough not to know, Esther the Wonder Pig is a pig who became an internet sensation. Two gay men who were living in an apartment somewhere in America adopted her when she was a baby, thinking she was a 'micro-pig' who would make a cute little pet. They weren't actually allowed to have pets in their flat and it turned out that Esther wasn't a micro-pig at all but a proper farm pig who in three years had grown into a massive 600lb porker. The two guys started a Facebook campaign to get another apartment where the pig could live with them: it went viral, and now they run an animal sanctuary on a farm in Canada.

Melanie fancied the Esther the Wonder Pig cruise and, in fairness, it did sound pretty ace. Esther had built up such a following over the years that her 'parents' Steve and Derek had started to have events built around the values they had followed since having Esther, primarily veganism, care for the environment, animal welfare and love for each other. They had held a successful cruise the year before and so based on the feedback that Melanie saw on social media we thought it would be a good thing to attend. We were expecting cooking classes and talks about veganism and it was sold as a voyage for the ecological, vegan betterment of the world. But when we got there, it felt like just a typical American cruise.

The ship was absolutely massive. It was eighteen stories high. Walking up to it was like walking up to a tower block. I couldn't help thinking, *Oh, for fuck's sake!* It looked like my worst nightmare. It looked like Benidorm on the water ... except it was full of very big Americans. In a way, that turned out to be an advantage, because I didn't have any of the problems of being recognised. This is because I am not big in America, even though everyone else seems to be. (See what I did there? You're welcome). And when we got to sea, a lot of my prejudices went and I just threw myself into it. We went to bingo (which we won), we went to all the shows, we even joined in with the sing-songs.

By the time you hit your fifties you are very cynical about being marketed to, and this cruise was so commercialised that it was ridiculous. They had monetised everything. We would sail into a port in a place like Belize, and the company that owned the cruise ship would have built the port and would also own all of the shops that were in it. You couldn't help but feel that you were being exploited.

One of the weirdest days came when we sailed into a port in Costa Rica. The tour reps told Melanie and me, 'Listen, just so that you know, it is a beach day today and there are three cruise ships coming in at the same time. Do you want to book a sun lounger?'

It sounded like Hell on Earth to me. The Organisation for Economic Co-operation and Development (OECD) says that by 2020, 75 per cent of the American population will be overweight or obese, and I reckon on our ship the percentages were considerably higher. The vast majority of our 8,000 American fellow passengers were morbidly obese, and I tried to imagine them all on the beach, multiplied by three, with no shirts on. It wasn't an attractive mental image. So, I asked the reps: 'Is there anywhere else we can go?'

'Well, there *is* a private beach,' they told us.

'Great! I don't care what it costs,' I told them, recklessly. 'We'll have a cabana on the private beach.'

We paid through the nose for the privilege and the ship docked near to the main beach. The sand was just 250 yards away, but that hadn't stopped them installing a chair lift to carry those who didn't want to walk to their sun loungers. The reps directed Melanie and I to a gate that led to the private beach. We walked through it and found ourselves on, at most, fifty square metres of sand ... directly underneath the chairlift.

It was the best offer we had going, so Melanie and I lay down on the sand. A minute later, there was what seemed like a total eclipse of the sun. I looked up to observe this astronomical phenomena, only to see a chair lift passing overhead with a massive American passenger in it. It set the tone for the day as every few minutes someone built like Homer Simpson passed over us and blocked out the light: sun, eclipse, sun, eclipse. It was beyond parody. Later that day, Melanie took a photo of me in a big rubber ring, floating in front of our tower-block cruise ship, thumbs up like I had won the perfect holiday in a raffle.

As you age, you relax your rigid views and find you don't mind things that you used to hate. I've always loathed being herded around, on holidays or anywhere, but as I'm getting older, I don't mind so much if a tour rep tells me, 'Go over there, stand there, point at that, take a photo, get back in the van.' I suppose it stops me having to think for myself. I can just tell them, 'Thank you, young man!'

It was different when I was younger but, now, I want a holiday to be a holiday – refreshing and relaxing. I used to come back from a holiday knackered. That is very much not the case now. I find myself saving a book to take with me on holiday, and when you're planning your reading material in advance, you know it's not going to be a mad one, because you are going to spend a lot of time sat on your arse reading.

I'm not sure I'll do another cruise, though. I want to get a lot more selective with my holidays, because the thing about getting older is that there are so many things I want to do and places I want to go, and there is less and less time left to do them. It's a mortality thing. Holidays become a barometer of whether you are managing to do the things that you said you would do in your life. They become much more important than they used to be, and the danger there is that you can over-invest in them.

Our Dream Holiday from Hell

For Melanie and me, the classic example of this came two years ago. It was our first proper holiday together with no kids, since we had just become empty-nesters, and we were going to Thailand for two weeks. Thailand is fantastic: I'm not surprised more than a third of a million Brits go there each year. The hotel had amazing views, it all looked perfect online, Melanie and I had invested in this holiday so much that we assumed it would be a rekindling of our old romantic life and the start of a new era ... and it was *absolutely shit*.

We had an argument on the first day. We were spending our first night in Bangkok before going on to our lovely hotel in Phuket. Melanie's grandad is buried by the River Kwai in Kanchanaburi, and we were going to spend a day going to see his grave. The hotel asked us if we wanted to use one of their cars, which was a big flash Mercedes, but I said to Melanie, 'That seems a bit wrong – turning up at a prisoner-of-war camp in a bloody Mercedes? Let's just get a taxi.'

'Well, we use Uber,' said the concierge.

'OK then, great, let's get an Uber,' I said

An Uber driver came along, picked us up, and – I don't have a clue how he managed to do this – drove us two-and-a-half hours in the wrong direction. I had no idea he had done it until I thought it was taking a very long time, glanced at my map, and saw he had taken us totally the wrong way. His one job was to get us there and back and he had totally messed it up. It took us forever to get there and when we got out of the car, I told him very emphatically, in a manner that did not require translation, to piss off.

Melanie and I went around the River Kwai cemetery, stopped to pay our respects at her grandad's grave, and did all the things that we wanted to do. When it came time to go back to the hotel, we asked at the office for a taxi number, only to be told that there wasn't one: 'No Uber here! No taxi!'

We walked to the local bus station and got on the bus to Bangkok. There were literally people with goats on there. I told Melanie, 'I'm sorry, but I can't do this all the way back to Bangkok!' and we got off again. In despair, I asked a random man at the bus terminal if he could help us to get a taxi. His eyes lit up. 'Yes, yes!' he told us. 'Follow me! Come, come!'

The man took us around the corner to the back of the bus station and proudly showed us an open-back truck with a load of people sitting in it. Either they were farm workers, or he was the most indiscreet people trafficker ever. I think they were farm workers. 'Get in there!' the fellow told me and Melanie. 'You what? No!' I said. 'No, I take you, I take you!' he managed, via some very broken English. 'I take you to taxi!'

Melanie and I didn't exactly have too many other options at this point, so we did. We got in and squatted on the low benches with all of the Thai agricultural workers. We left Kanchanaburi and we went off bumping down a series of remote country roads, bouncing off the potholes. By now I was more convinced than ever that this was a terrible idea, and Melanie was fuming. Clearly, she thought I could have organised this one a tad better. I am pretty sure she was casting her mind back longingly to that flash hotel Mercedes.

One by one, the agricultural workers all got off at various stops until only Melanie and I were left in the back of the pick-up. At this point the driver turned off the main road and went down into a tiny village. He headed towards a tatty old garage, at which point warning bells were going off in my head big-time. I had no reason to trust him and I had no idea what, or who, was waiting for us in that ropey garage.

'Whatever happens here, don't get out,' I whispered to Melanie. 'If he opens the door, and there's a lot of fellas in there, I will try to do what I can – but don't you get out!'

The truck stopped. I climbed down from the back, trying to work out how I could look threatening enough for all of the waiting assailants to leave us alone. I clenched my fists as the driver went into the garage, fully expecting him to reappear with a gang, or a Samurai sword, or both, to rob us of whatever cash we had on us. Instead, he came out grinning proudly and carrying car keys. He took the cover off a car that was standing nearby. It looked like a Skoda. 'Get in, get in!' he beamed, and drove us all the way to Bangkok.

It had been quite a day and it did not get any better that night. When Melanie was trying to find her way to the bathroom, she kicked a table and managed to break her foot. We had to go off to a Bangkok hospital and get her foot put in a cast, then head to the airport (her fracture turned out to be quite an advantage there, as it meant we missed all of the airport queues). She had to get lifted into the plane and off we went for Phuket, to the posh hotel we had booked that everybody said was amazing. Well, it was amazing – but it was also in a very hilly bit of Phuket and Melanie was in a wheelchair or on crutches, which was a pain in the arse.

It seemed like things on our dream holiday could really not get any worse. Then the part of Thailand we were in got hit by the worst monsoon it had had in seventy-five years. When the heavens opened, it pissed down like I had never seen before. Melanie and I started bitching about how much time and money and effort we had invested in this fucking awful holiday. We turned on the TV for a little light relief. 'This monsoon is very serious,' the English-language news channel told us. 'It has wiped out villages. It has killed eighteen people.'

Your holiday might be a bit shit but when villages are being washed away, you gain a new perspective. Nothing is that important. We just decided to make the most of the time we had left on holiday. Melanie and I had ten days left in Thailand and the monsoon was predicted to last for another eight. We were in desperate need of a Plan B and, luckily, I came up with one that I figured might just salvage the holiday. We were due to fly home via Dubai so I looked online for alternative stays. A car drive from Dubai, in Oman, I found a gorgeous-looking hotel in a peaceful place we had been to before called Zighy Bay. It was a cool, groovy eco-hotel next to a village that had been there for 1,500 years. Perfect!

The plan worked like a dream ... for one night. We flew to Dubai, drove to Oman and settled in to the hotel. The first night there was beautiful. The next night, it got a little bit windy. Then it got more than a little bit windy. It transpired that every hundred years or so, a freak of nature happens in Zighy Bay whereby the ocean wind that passes the bay diverts into the bay itself. In no time at all, a full-blown hurricane was raging around us. There was no way we could do anything at all but bunker down in the hotel and take cover.

By now we were sat in the third five-star hotel we had stayed in on this doomed trip. Melanie had broken her foot in the first one, we had got flooded out of the second one, and when we woke up in the third one on the morning after the hurricane, the palm trees were down and so were all the means of communication.

It was supposed to have been our holiday of a lifetime but had been an utter fiasco from start to finish. Really, it would have been better to have just gone to Benidorm. We did see the funny side of it, eventually, but it was a close thing. The only plus point to the week spent indoors avoiding natural disasters was that I managed to finish Bruce Springsteen's autobiography, which was as much of an epic as one of his shows – you have to lock yourself away for a few days to even think of attempting it.

As you get older, you have to accept that your idea of a good holiday changes. You find yourself yearning for a bit of peace and quiet and there is nothing wrong with that. As I head into my pensionable years, I suspect life will go full circle and I'll go back to soaking up the sun in Majorca, like I used to thirty years ago. But where I used to stagger in pissed-up from clubbing at 6am, now I'll be getting up at precisely the same time to put my towel down on a deck chair.

7.

HOW TO STAY FIT AND STILL LOVE SPORT

ONE OBVIOUS THING ABOUT getting older is that your relationship with sport will change simply because you physically cannot do the things you used to do. Sport becomes like sex – something you have more chance of watching someone doing well than actually doing it well yourself.

It is important to stay fit, however, so you can at least still play sport – and us middle-aged men are trying to do so. Today, there are more than 7,000 gyms in the UK with a total membership of nearly ten million, which means that one person in seven is a member of a gym. A large percentage of them are over forty-five.

One reason for this, of course, is that there are more people over forty-five alive than ever before, and we expect to stay healthy for longer. As I said earlier, it is also impossible to visit social media without being informed that some celebrity or fitness guru is currently *hashtag smashing it!* in the gym. I am definitely one of those middle-aged people who feels the need to stay fit.

I have always maintained a reasonable level of fitness but in recent years the way I have done that has had to change. This is partly as a result of the physical limitations my body is putting on me, and partly due to the change in my life with work and getting older. When I was a kid, if I wanted to play football I would go to the street with a ball, knock on a few doors and find a dozen or so other lads to play football with. Try doing that when you are fifty-two and you are likely to end up with a restraining order.

I am interested in *why* we grow old and change. Take professional footballers. They have been supreme athletes all their adult lives and have been looked after by the top physiotherapists, sports scientists, nutritionists and doctors. And yet at a certain age even the best of them have to stop. Even Lionel Messi won't go on forever. Somehow, the aging process has robbed them of their powers and they become ordinary (unless, of course, you play against them in a charity football game, and realise they are still a million times better than you).

As a human being, you reach your physical peak, usually sometime in your twenties, and then you have to live the rest of your life – the vast majority of it, in fact – in decline. It doesn't seem fair. It would be great if we could grow more powerful as we got older and die when we are at our best, not be good when we are young then spend seventy years trying to remember what it was that we were once good at.

I reckon the octopus has got it right. The male octopus lives long enough to find a mate and have sex. After that, his work is done and he dies. The female octopus then lays the eggs and sits on them, brooding, until they hatch. When the baby octopuses swim away, the mother's work is done and she also dies.

It seems a perfect trade-off. The octopuses live long enough to be a fit enough adult to attract a mate, have sex, lay eggs and hatch them and die. They have none of the hassle of bringing up the kids, no risk of their relationship becoming stale and boring, and no wasted time thinking they could have done so much better with their octopoid lives. They are here for one purpose, they achieve it, and they shuffle off this mortal coil.

As most octopuses only live for one or two years, I suppose they can't really expect to do all that much more with their lives. However, one octopus has set a new record for the longest brooding period for any species. A few years ago, scientists from the Monterey Bay Aquarium Research Institute (MBARI) revealed that they had watched a deep-sea octopus called *Graneledone boreopacifica* guard its eggs for four-and-a-half years – the longest known brooding period of any animal on the planet. As most octopuses only live for half as long as that, this meant that the *Graneledone boreopacifica* is also the octopus which lived the longest. Amazingly, over the course of the octopus's fifty-three-month brooding period, the researchers never saw her eat, even when they tried to offer her food. This obviously had an impact on her, and the researchers watched as she grew paler, lost weight, her skin sagged and her eyes grew cloudy. This merely tells me that sitting on eggs until they hatch has the same effect on you as having children and bringing them up.

Having first identified the octopus and seen her brooding on eggs in May 2007, the research team made a total of eighteen visits over four-and-a-half years and each time she had not moved. At some point between September and October 2011, the eggs hatched and the mother left, presumably to die somewhere feeling that she had done all that was expected of her. At no time during the period that the researchers watched the aging octopus did they note she had a gym membership card or was doing eight-armed press-ups with a personal trainer.

The *Graneledone boreopacifica* did what human beings used to do before we complicated life with thoughts and ambition. It was born, became an adult, fulfilled its natural role on earth of reproducing, then died. Human beings are the only species that not only questions its own mortality but also wants to challenge that mortality by remaining as young as it can for as long as it can.

Why Do We Get Old?

What is the aging process, and why do we get old? The first thing that is clear is nobody is 100 per cent certain why we, and every other living organism, age. When you think about it, we accept mortality as an inevitable part of life, and the end of it. Yet from a simplistic point of view it seems unnecessary – why can't we simply go on for ever?

One of the best explanations of how and why we age comes from the American Federation of Aging Research. Their researchers have begun to reach consensus about aging, which it has been accepted for years is caused by cells not replicating as well as you get older. They say that when chromosomes divide, a cap-like feature at the end called a telomere gets shorter with each replication process, and it appears this reduces the ability of the cells to divide and generate new, healthier cells.

Humans have increased their average life span through innovations such as antibiotics and better sanitation, but at the level of human DNA, there is something happening which appears to be beyond our control. Basically, we age because nature made us that way and there is only a slim chance that science will every fully understand why it happens, let alone slow it down.

Even experiments that have shown some success in trying to slow down the aging process at a cellular level in mice, fruit flies and roundworms have had their own problems. If it has been achieved through methods such as a calorie-deficient diet or single-gene mutation, the animal that lives longer does so at the expense of reduced fertility, among other potential side effects.

I am simplifying the science considerably here but actually I love the simplicity of the message. You are here for a fixed period of time. You may extend it a little by staying fit, but Mother Nature has built a ticking clock inside of every living creature and at some point, its time will be up. If you try to tinker with it and extend the life span of any creature, Mother Nature reduces that creature's ability to replicate, so over time that creature could become extinct. It's a blunt message: cope with the hand Mother Nature has dealt you.

On that cheery note, we have to accept that we are born into a body that will over time become less healthy and efficient. It's the natural decay of an organic entity. The big difference between us and other organic entities such as trees is that nobody is showing trees pictures of other trees, and asking, 'Why haven't *you* got branches like that?' We would probably all feel better in our own skin if we didn't think that there was a better version of growing old knocking about somewhere.

If we are to make the most of our aging bodies for fitness or sport, we need to know what is going to happen to us as we grow older. I decided to seek out a bit of professional advice on the aging process and what is going to happen, so turned to the wealth of free information from the NHS. This is an institution that was set up to realise the vision of William Beveridge, set out in a 1942 report, that the government should establish a social security system that would take care of its citizens 'from the cradle to the grave'. This is still the aim of the NHS, even though in many ways it is a victim of its own success: the well-documented pressures placed upon it come in part because we are living longer and taking more resources before we reach 'the grave'.

Since its inception in 1948, the NHS has helped to raise the age of life expectancy in the UK by an average thirteen years and it has also saved many people who may not have been treated in a different system, myself included. When I was ten years old the existence of the NHS saved my life. I had complained about a pain in my left leg for weeks but the GP was convinced it was due to torn ligaments from playing football, so insisted the best treatment was to bandage the left knee. This only seemed to increase the pain and so my mum insisted I was seen in a hospital. When this was done the X-rays and other investigations led to an emergency operation to treat an infection in my left femur called osteomyelitis. This was explained to my parents as being like having an abscess inside my bone that was ready to burst. The process of bandaging the leg tightly only served to cause more pain as it applied more pressure to the site of the infection.

The doctors warned my parents that, firstly, they would do their best to operate before the infection went systemic, which could prove fatal. Secondly they would hope to save my leg but could not guarantee they could. And, thirdly, if they did save the leg, it may not grow at the same rate as the right leg and so lifelong complications would potentially follow. The operation was a success and after a few months in hospital and three years of follow up I was completely discharged, when it was clear that my legs were growing at the same rate. Had we lived in a fee-paying or insurance-based system, I am pretty sure I would not have had the same level of care and might well be looking at the world on a slant.

I have also been on the other side of the NHS system when a mistake was made due to the workload and pressure that everyone working within the system suffers under. Three years ago I had a persistent cough that I could not shake. I put it down the usual bugs you pick up when travelling and touring, but even a course of antibiotics failed to shift it. After twelve weeks with no sign of the cough going, the GP sent me for a chest X-ray. I was told that unless I heard anything, I should regard everything as normal and the cough would go. I heard nothing and gradually my chest cleared, so I thought no more about it. Three months later I received a call from my GP. He said that the results of the X-ray had been misreported by one of the junior staff. I had in fact had a shadow on both lungs and he was putting me forward for an emergency CT scan to investigate further, which would take a few days to organise unless I wanted to pay to expedite it. Something in his tone suggested to me that getting it done sooner than later would be the best idea, so I organised a private CT scan in the local hospital.

I spent a few hours alone thinking that it could be the start of the end. This is because I am a man and we are always dramatic, and also because a Google search of 'shadows on both lungs' does not make you believe the prognosis will be good. It was the first time I had seriously contemplated my own death and I was obviously filled with sadness for all the things I would miss: the healthy years ahead of me that I had planned to enjoy, my sons getting married, becoming a grandparent, laughing, blue sky, days when you are so happy that you almost feel guilty to be so lucky, waking up feeling safe, holding Melanie's hand, being with mates, football, music, films I love and those I would never see, books I love and those I would never read, arriving somewhere new, the sound of children laughing, the feeling when you make strangers laugh, my parents, my brother, my sisters and their families, Christmas, sex, walking the dogs, being rained on, seeing my breath in the cold, being too hot in the sun … The list could go on. Death takes away everything, although this isn't all bad: I suddenly realised I did not have to care anymore about what Donald Trump did, if the ice caps were going to melt and if the recent Brexit vote was as problematic as I thought it might be. (I got that one right!)

I was potentially dying and everything external to me became immediately less important. I had seen this before with people facing terminal illness. There is a sense of contentment and balance that is hard to explain, given that they know they are dying. For a few hours I understood. It is the state of mind you can only achieve when you focus on what is important and leave the rest behind; the petty stresses of modern life disappear when you consider you may be dying and all that matters are those you love. Melanie came with me for my scan and though we were both nervous she was struck by my new serenity. Whatever was to be the diagnosis we would face it together.

The GP called me as soon as he had the results. The scan revealed that I did have shadows on both lungs but that it was not cancer or anything sinister, but was instead caused by increased calcification in my sternum. They thought I had obviously hurt it at some point, along with my ribs, although there was nothing in my medical records saying when this happened. I revealed to the GP that I had no memory of anything that could have caused it; in fact, I only recall hurting my chest significantly once when I was a child and a friend dared me to do a belly flop off a high wall. I took up the challenge and remember my chest hurt when I landed and continued to do so when I walked home – but nothing on the scale of a broken sternum! Still, whatever the reason for the increased bone mass in my chest, I put the phone down grateful for the life I had ahead of me. All the joy I thought I would never have again began to flood my body. I told Melanie, embraced her and then on the radio in the background I heard Donald Trump was saying global warming was a myth, and I started worrying again.

If I was going to carry on living, I thought I may as well learn the best way to do it, so did a bit of research into the information the NHS offered: in particular, a helpful guide called *A Practical Guide to Healthy Ageing*. I decided it would be neighbourly to pass on some of the things I learned.

1. YOUR BONES AND MUSCLES WILL NO LONGER HELP YOU LIKE YOU WANT THEM TO

The NHS website tells us that our bones are going to lose strength as we get older, but has lots of helpful advice on helping to prevent fractures and falls:

- Keep active. Even taking the stairs rather than the lift can help you build strong bones and slow bone loss, but other activities suggested include bike-riding, tennis or pushing a lawn mower. The NHS particularly suggests 'moderate-intensity' exercise – the way to tell if you're doing it is if you can still talk but can't sing the words to a song (this test isn't as helpful if your memory is failing and you can't remember the words to any songs). Ballroom and line dancing are also suggested as examples of moderate-intensity exercise, in case you had a sequinned shirt or cowboy hat lying around that you wanted to put to good use.
- Eat plenty of calcium. Apparently our appetites can start to drop as we get older (I'm yet to see evidence of this) but, even if we don't feel like eating much, a healthy diet is still very important.

Calcium is particularly crucial, making our bones (and teeth) strong and rigid. In the UK, the recommended amount of calcium for an adult is 700 milligrams, but the amount we need increases as we get older. You can get calcium from dairy products, soya, green leafy vegetables, tofu, fish or nuts.

- Neck plenty of vitamin D, too. This helps with absorption of calcium. We are supposed to get most of the vitamin D we need from the sun, but as we live in the UK where the sun unfortunately likes to play a constant game of hide and seek, we're all advised to consider taking a supplement. Other good sources include oily fish, eggs and fortified breakfast cereals.

2. YOUR HEART IS GOING TO NEED SOME EXTRA HELP

As we age, we all know that most important muscle in our body becomes less and less efficient, but the advice to give your heart a fighting chance is pretty obvious: simply do what you know you should.

To keep your heart in shape, you should do the following:

- Don't smoke
- Exercise
- Stick to a healthy weight
- Eat well, with more fibre and fish, less saturated fat and salt – but get your five-a-day.
- Drink less alcohol
- Reduce stress

Of all the advice available, this was the area that surprised me the most because it was so obvious. There was nothing there I had never heard before and I am sure everyone else will know all this too. You have to be a bit of an idiot to not be aware that these things are what you should be doing. I think the NHS should start a campaign called 'Don't be a tit – and it will help your heart'.

3. YOUR EYES, EARS AND TEETH START THINKING YOU DON'T NEED THEM

It would seem obvious that your eyes and your ears are going to deteriorate because – why wouldn't they? Everything else is! However, there are simple steps that we can take:

- Have regular eye tests, particularly as these can pick up eye diseases such as glaucoma and cataracts. You should also have your hearing tested regularly.
- Again, eat a balanced diet, stay active and sleep well. Not just useful for your overall health, this can help with some eye conditions too.
- Strong sunlight can damage your eyes, so wear sunglasses to protect them, and consider wearing earplugs if you are going to be around loudspeakers, machinery or Brian Blessed. This is great advice and explains why so many cool older people wear sunglasses. I can't wait to start wearing a sombrero with sunglasses everywhere I go, and nobody will be able to say anything because I will be old.
- Brush your teeth at least twice a day, floss and do not let vegetation grow in your teeth unchecked. If you do not take care of your teeth gums can recede and you will end up with teeth that belong on zombie – not a good look. Apparently, this

happens to your teeth even if you have trademarked them, as I have. My teeth are by far the best part of me. If they ever fall out, I will take it as a similar signal to the octopus's eggs hatching, and know that my time here is done.

4. YOUR DIGESTIVE SYSTEM WILL GO ON STRIKE AND YOUR BLADDER WILL BECOME A LEAKY SPONGE

This was something that did surprise me. I guess it's an aspect of aging that I had not considered, although apparently 2.5 million people in the UK over the age of sixty experience bladder problems, often without telling anyone (which makes you wonder who came up with that number if they don't tell anyone – but that's statistics for you). There is a number of things you can do to help:

- Don't hold off on the water! The advice says not to cut down on liquids if you suffer with incontinence as that can make it worse, which I simply cannot work out – surely less in means less out – but if that is what the NHS says then you have to believe it.
- Limit caffeine – the caffeine in tea and coffee can make your symptoms worse, so having less of it will help to reduce incontinence. This potentially gives decaf coffee producers a whole new marketing spin – 'drink decaf and avoid wearing incontinence pads.' Not the coolest strapline ever, and I am not sure what the advert would look like, but there is obviously a market there.
- Pelvic floor exercises (otherwise known as Kegel exercises) will help – as I learnt from various sources. A Google search

on what exactly these involved yielded a very entertaining few minutes, when I found a YouTube clip of a doctor explaining them. Within a few sentences, this doctor had said virtually every word that would have made my twelve-year-old self blush and laugh in sex education classes at school: rectum, labia, vagina, vaginal wall, penis, squirt and drip. She even used the memorable phrase, 'You want to bring the turtle head back into the shop' to explain how the penis should contract during a Kegel exercise. I have no idea when this doctor made the video, and what her intended audience was, but I am grateful. As a middle-aged man, I am glad I have a better understanding of what I need to do and, as a comedian, I am glad she gave me the opportunity to giggle like a twelve-year-old boy again.

- Waiting to take a number two can cause constipation – the other surprise I learnt from some of the advice I read. When you've gotta go, you've gotta go.

This last is the piece of advice that shocked me the most. I don't recall anyone ever informing me that delaying a toilet trip can cause constipation and, as soon as my bowels want to release, I should do so regardless of the situation I am in. I can see some awkward moments ahead, but it does validate everything Miriam Margoyles said.

5. YOUR SKIN BECOMES BAGGY

Now, this *is* bad news. You probably won't be surprised to learn this, as it's not something that's as easy for an older person to hide as more infrequent bowel movements, but these are the things you can do to promote healthy skin:

- Cover up with clothes that protect your skin from the sun and apply sunscreen
- Not smoke or drink too much
- Use mild soaps and moisturiser
- Check your skin regularly and tell your doctor if you see any changes

I must admit, to know that one day you will have far more skin than you will really need or want is always going to be slightly depressing, particularly when it is clear that as you grow older it is harder to remain slim because your metabolism slows down to that of a hibernating tortoise, so that even looking at a cake makes you put on weight. This continues to emphasise the importance of exercise, but it feels like your body is doing its best to wind you up – as you get fatter, your skin becomes baggier, so that you will never reach your own edge. You are like the universe and constantly expanding.

6. YOUR SEXUALITY IS GOING TO BE DIFFERENT IN THAT IT MAY NOT INCLUDE ANY ACTUAL SEX

I guess sex in the elderly has always been going on, but finding it is like finding the Christian name of your school teacher – even though you kind of know it exists, it's still strange to see it written down in front of you.

The NHS advice is to accept that the sex drive of you or your partner may well change over time and that you should embrace the change. This may mean that intercourse is replaced with other sexual activities, particularly when one or the other may be less physically able. There is even a section about how to have sex when one or both of you has arthritis. Little tips like taking painkillers before sex could change everything for some couples, as could the advice to use 'pillows or adaptive equipment for support'.

However, the one piece of advice I saw with regard to intimacy that I thought was possibly off-target was the tip to have a bath or shower together. Considering a number of elderly people will have one of those adapted baths with a door in that you walk into, close and then fill with water, I cannot imagine how that would enhance the moment. You both walk in naked, with your big bodies and baggy skin, and sit down and close the door. Then sitting face-to-face you turn the taps and sit while your bath fills with water. One of you will inevitably be closer to the hot water tap, which is bound to cause some resentment. Then, as you sit looking at each other while water fills, you will have to have some form of conversation – perhaps sexy-talk like, 'You have no idea what I going to do to you once these bubbles come …' When the bath is full you can turn the taps off, play footsy and then when you're done you can pull the plug and continue looking at each other while the water drains to the point where it is low enough for you to open the door and step out, one after the other – which you will want to do as you will both be getting cold. Somehow, I think what is meant to be good advice needs to be more specific to say the instruction does not include baths with doors in because they are passion-killers.

7. YOU NEED TO LOOK AFTER WHAT IS INSIDE YOUR SKULL

We all expect, to a greater or lesser extent, that our mental capabilities will reduce as we get older. This is just a part of the natural process of our body not being what it once was. But with dementia and Alzheimer's disease being so prevalent, forgetting where you put your keys or someone's name can induce an element of fear that is probably unnecessary. To look after your brain, you have to do all the standard things listed in other sections – exercise and maintain a healthy diet and weight – but it's also important to keep up with some specific things to preserve the health of your brain:

- Diet, exercise, not drinking too much – all the same advice from other sections applies here too.
- Keep your heart healthy. Some studies have shown that up to 80 per cent of patients suffering from dementia also suffer from cardiovascular disease.
- Make sure to get enough sleep, including a daytime nap if you need one. As discussed in previous chapters, this is something I'm very much on-board with.
- Keep your mind busy. This seems to be the most important thing you can do. It isn't necessarily doing things like crosswords, because that is trying to get the brain to recall something it already knows; what you need to do is create new challenges for the brain by trying to learn something new.

The famous 'Nun Study', which was started by researcher David Snowden in 1986 and is still ongoing, studied the cognitive ability of nearly 700 nuns in the United States. The nuns range in age between 75 and 103, and what makes the study so useful is the uniformity of the study population. All the nuns have a similar lifestyle, share a gender, have similar (minimal) alcohol consumption patterns and do not smoke. They represent a uniform cohort with a similar baseline and all agreed to annual blood assessments, cognitive testing, physical and medical examinations throughout the study and even donated their brains upon death. What has been striking about the study is that it is yielding some results that suggest the physical deterioration of the brain (that may suggest the person would be suffering from signs of cognitive decline) has not always manifested itself as would be expected. Indeed some of the brains that have belonged to the 'brightest' of the nuns have appeared the most damaged upon autopsy.

To date the nun study suggests that linguistic ability provides some protection against dementia or cognitive deterioration. Researchers have suggested this may be because a wider vocabulary or a linguistic ability with other languages creates more synapses in the brain, as it can find alternative routes to understand what it is confronted with.

For example, if you see a photograph of Jürgen Klopp (I apologise; this was the first example that came to mind) and know he is the manager of Liverpool, you have one piece of information to understand who the person in the picture is. But let's say you see a picture of Jürgen Klopp and you think:

1. He's the manager of Liverpool.
2. He is a German football manager.
3. He managed the team that won the Champions League in 2019.
4. He managed a team in Germany called Dortmund.
5. He is a football manager with good teeth.
6. He is a German man who lives in Liverpool and likes wearing baseball caps.

7. His surname rhymes with 'hop'.

8. His Christian name rhymes with 'Bergen'.

You see that instead of having one route to trying to recognise the person in the picture you have eight, or as many as you can think of, and if you throw in knowing another language you have immediately expanded the routes you will go through to find the answer to 'who is that?' or 'what is that?'

The advice from the NHS, and virtually every other source in the world, is to keep the brain active, but also within the NHS advice is the area that I had genuinely not considered, that of mental health rather than mental ability. Good mental wellbeing can be so much harder when you reach an age when partners, family and friends die, and without a workplace to go to you can quickly become isolated and depressed. The NHS advice involves keeping in touch with family, making arrangements with friends or planning to be involved in social groups. All good standard tips, but the advice in the *A Practical Guide to Healthy Ageing* pamphlet has, on the top of the list on the page titled 'Look after your mental health': 'Begin a conversation – Communication is key to wellbeing and we all respond to a friendly face.'

I thought about this a lot when I read it. We are telling the older members of our society to start the conversation, to walk up to someone and *start the conversation*. How hard is that to do? How many times have we, in our busy lives, smiled at the old person who tried to talk to us, given them a quick response and moved on? How many of us have reversed this and started the conversation with an older person sat on their own? This is the thing I have taken from this book, to start the conversation with someone older whenever I see them alone; you never know what you will learn. The last time I did this was in a more formal situation, when I was sat next to a lady on a flight back from Mallorca. We had booked the seats too late for Melanie and me to sit together, so I found myself sat next to a woman who looked like she was in her late-sixties or early-seventies.

We exchanged the usual nod and 'hello', as you do when you sit next to a stranger on a flight and I settled to watch something on my ipad, but after twenty-five minutes or so, for some reason, I took my headphones off and we started a conversation. She was with her husband who was sat on the front row. They had been forced to sit separately because he was travelling with a nurse. They had been on a cruise and he 'had taken a turn', and after a couple of weeks in a Spanish hospital they were now returning for him to be treated at home. He kept looking back and putting a thumbs up, as she explained that they had been married for over sixty years. He was in his early nineties and she was in her eighties.

I said all the things you would imagine about how great it was that they remained married and that I genuinely would not have thought she was in her eighties, which was all true. Then she told me a little piece of magic: 'I can't imagine being without him, but we both know it will happen – so we keep going on holiday so that we are not sat at home waiting for it.' She continued, 'I never used to feel old. You hear people saying they are old when they are forty: that's nonsense. I didn't feel old when I turned forty, or fifty, or sixty, or seventy. It was eighty ... that's when you feel old!'

If entering your ninth decade on the planet is when you start to feel old, I will take that!

So, there you go: some sterling advice from our beloved National Health Service. I felt like a lot of what the guide said centred on the fact that you can't stop the aging process but you can prepare for it and make your life better. It's just like PE at school. It's something that is good for you even if you don't necessarily want to do it. And, ultimately, a note from your mum getting you out of it is only cheating yourself, and you may be forced to do it in your underwear anyway.

Anfield of Dreams

Once we accept that sport and physical activity are good for us, the question is which sport to play. When you're young, your exposure to sport is all about where you come from. For me, as a kid, it was always about football. In school sports lessons the teachers would just throw us a football and leave us to it. I'm not even sure we had a school cricket team. I had a great PE teacher, Mr Hilton, who knew we were all about football and nothing else. Another teacher tried to introduce rugby, but somebody broke their arm on the first day we played it, and someone else broke their collarbone the next. That was the end of that.

We would play football at school, and we'd play it in the street after school, and it was the big point of connection between me, my dad and my brother, Eddie. We had a very male-dominated house in terms of when the football was on. My mum and my sisters would go out in the kitchen and the three of us would sit and watch the match. I suppose it was a way of lads being together.*

---

* *That would not happen now. I think my sister Kathy is probably a bigger Liverpool fan than I am.*

Where I was from, everybody I knew supported Liverpool or Everton (or, very rarely, Tranmere Rovers – until my brother played for them, and then we all supported them). We were a Liverpool house. We'd mostly watch the games on the telly, which really meant highlights, as live games were rare in those days, unless it was the FA Cup final or the World Cup.

A few times a year, my dad would take me to Anfield, which was always a big event. I was lucky as a kid because that was the period when Liverpool were winning everything. That changed when I got into my early twenties, and it's only started changing back lately.

There were some amazing players at Liverpool when I was first going to see them but, oddly enough, the most skilful players were never my favourites. That might be something to do with the kind of player that I turned out to be. In my twenties I played non-league, semi-professional football, primarily in the Northern Premier League. We were part of the pyramid system that could lead to league football but you would have to get promoted to the Vauxhall Conference and win that before progressing to the Fourth Division.*

I was never going to reach the dizzy heights of full professionalism because I had limited ability and I lacked pace. About my august career, my Wikipedia entry says only this: *'Bishop ... was known for having an aggressive style of play.'* Now, not everything you read on Wikipedia is true. But *that* probably is. I made up

---

* *The Fourth Division is now League Two. When the First Division became the Premier League, and the Second Division became the Championship, the Fourth Division became League Two, which I suppose sounds better for the teams that are languishing there. It is like the football industry has learnt from the clothes industry and changed the labels to make everyone feel better.*

for my lack of skill by putting in more effort – in fact, a little less effort and a little more skill would not have gone amiss. There is a joke there about love-making, but I just can't bring myself to make it.

When I grew up, Liverpool had a brilliant team with the star player being Kevin Keegan, but I was drawn to Ian Callaghan, Jimmy Case and Terry McDermott – the midfield engine room. Kenny Dalglish came along and he was a totally unbelievable player, but I was still drawn to Sammy Lee, Graeme Souness, Jan Molby and Ronnie Whelan, perhaps because Dalglish was so far ahead as a player there was no point in me even trying to emulate him as a kid. I suppose I always liked the players who did the hard work that let the great players shine. And then we got Steven Gerrard, who was so good that he did both.

It's the same for me even today. I see Liverpool players like Virgil van Dijk and Mo Salah, and they are unbelievably good. But if you ask me the ones I look for in the squad, and who make a difference to the team, it is people like James Milner. You always know what you're getting from him when he starts, and when he comes on as a sub, he affects the game. People like him and Jordan Henderson are the glue that holds the team together.

Of course, as you get older, the way you watch football changes, as does your whole relationship with sport. When I was in my twenties, I was playing matches myself most Saturdays so I couldn't watch Liverpool so much and my own matches were more important to me. I figured that if Liverpool were not taking a Saturday off to come up to see me play at Southport, I wouldn't take a Saturday off to see them.

I suppose a small part of me probably thought I could be playing for Liverpool, stupid as that was. That's how you change. When you're in your twenties, *you can do everything*, and you just have to decide what things to do. When you're in your fifties, you're glad to do *anything*. Getting older, you learn your limitations and you develop an appreciation for those who can do things better than you. Sport, art, music, acting, pub quizzes – anything that looks easy until you try it and realise it is beyond your capability. It doesn't mean you don't have some skills: it's just that you don't necessarily have the skills you would like.

Now I'm fifty-two, I've accepted my limitations. I am probably never going to learn to play the piano that I bought in order to learn to play the piano. I am never going to be good at pub quizzes because I made a decision a long time ago to only keep things in my brain that I might find useful, so I am never going to keep random facts in it.

I am the same with football trivia. I have loads of mates who can pull football facts out of the air. My sons Danny and Joe can do it, and my brother Eddie loves a football quiz, but ask me about who played in a certain game and what the score was and I will not have a clue, even if I was at the game. I don't have head space for that stuff, so even in pub quizzes, when people expect me to have the answers to football questions, I don't know.

I have also accepted that I am never going to play for Liverpool. This did not just happen now I am fifty-two: I am not deluded. I think I probably accepted it by the time I was thirty-seven. This has meant I am now more committed to watching them. I suppose it's like if you go to see somebody in a play, or you see a piece of art, and you think, *I could never have done that*. It makes you appreciate it more. That comes with age, because with age, you start learning your own limitations. But I have also had regret that I have not made the most of my talents and become the best at something.

This could have been a lesser contested sport such as pole-vaulting. Right now, in the UK there is someone who is the best pole-vaulter in the whole country and hardly anybody knows who they are.* Yet that would have been enough for me: just knowing I was the best. It could have been the world record for eating jam on toast: anything that validates you as the best, if only for a short time.

Supporting a football team gives you a strange emotional investment. It means you love something that you can't influence. It is not a balanced relationship because you will be let down, nobody will ask you what you think and, regardless of how much you are let down, the other party in the relationship knows you will not leave. However, the rewards of being a fan far outweigh all of that. I realise now that when Liverpool Football Club does well, there's a little sprinkle of happiness that falls on millions of people. The city does well and the perception of the city improves. The welfare of the people just seems that little bit better. It feels like so much more than just football.

When it comes to Liverpool, we've been through Hillsborough and Heysel and everything else. We understand the context of football in the harshest of terms. If you take all of those extreme situations out, the importance of Liverpool doing well now seems greater to me than it used to. It used to feel a little bit optional, whereas now it feels essential we do well. I never thought of it like that until the last five or ten years. It's the kind of thing that starts occurring to you as you grow old.

---

* *At the time of writing, it is Luke Cutts and Holly Bradshaw. So, well done you two.*

Champions League 2019

At the grand old age of fifty-two, I got totally immersed in Liverpool's Champions League adventures this year. But it wasn't until I was sitting in the Nou Camp just before the start of the first leg of the semi-final against Barcelona that I thought, *We could actually win this. We could win the whole thing.*

I had missed previous opportunities to see Liverpool play at the Nou Camp but this time I had the added incentives of the match falling on the day my friend Adam turned fifty and a desire to see Barcelona play with Lionel Messi, the best player of his generation, in the side. On the day of the match, we got to Barcelona and had a few drinks and I took him to a swanky members' club, Soho House, for lunch. We had some wine, and then we had some more wine, and then I said to Adam: 'Let's go upstairs! There's a pool on the roof, and we can survey the vista of Barcelona!' So we went upstairs, where there were supermodels types and cool people lounging around, and ... we fell asleep on the sun loungers around the pool. It was always going to happen. Two blokes in their fifties, with Liverpool FC scarves around their necks, snoring their heads off. I woke up with a dry mouth, two hours later, knowing we had completely pulled the status of the place down.

A few hours later at the Nou Camp, the game was a disaster. Sometimes you have to be careful what you wish for because Lionel Messi took over and we lost 3–0. As I sat with all of the Liverpool supporters at the end, waiting for the police to let us out of the ground, I thought we had no chance of going through. I decided it was all over, but I had been there and that was enough.

For the return leg at Anfield I had picked up a bit of a cold. I had some television commitments that I could not miss and didn't want to risk losing my voice so I gave my tickets for the second leg to my brother Eddie and son Daniel. The second leg turned out to be one of the epic European nights and I could easily have been pissed off that I missed it, particularly as I didn't even watch it live on the TV.

I was staying in a rented house in Sussex and had never even thought to check if it had BT Sport. I just assumed it would have. I built my whole day around watching the second leg, and come kick-off time I sat down, turned on the TV ... and BT Sport wasn't there. I couldn't just subscribe to it, because the subscription wasn't in my name, and I couldn't get hold of the landlord to ask him to do it.

What should I do? I was wondering, should I go to someone else's to watch it? Then I thought, oh, you know what? We're getting beat anyway! What's the point? I'll just go back to the 1970s and listen to the game on the radio. I'll pretend I've got a feather cut and I'm wearing flares and a three-star jumper. So, I sat in a chair, listening to Five Live, and it was absolutely brilliant.

The excitement, the roars ... it was totally unbelievable, especially when we got the fourth goal to go through. I can honestly say that it is the best time I have ever had at a football match that I didn't go to. Listening to that semi-final second leg on the radio genuinely felt as good as actually being there. Although speaking to everyone who *was* there afterwards that might be an exaggeration. But one thing is certain: I would definitely have lost my voice had I gone.

I went to Madrid for the final, when we beat Tottenham 2–0. It was a terrible game but I was so tense and caught up in it that by the end, I was absolutely exhausted. I was drained. The relief that I felt was quite unbelievable: I mean, there are so many other things in the world that I'd like to go well, and that are more important, but getting middle-aged doesn't mean you stop caring about big football matches. Quite the opposite.

This Is Anfield

One of the few good things about getting older, in relation to sport, is that you can most likely afford to watch it in greater comfort, if you want to. Yet that doesn't mean it will be more enjoyable. My dad, Eddie and I had always watched Liverpool from the terraces, and later from the stands, but one of the first things that I did when I broke through and got some money was buy us a luxury all-in match-day package at Anfield. It was the full works: going into the ground through the directors' entrance, a wander around the trophy room, and a posh pre-match three-course meal in what was then the Main Stand.

We did that for a season, and after it finished, I said to my dad and my brother, 'Well, what do you think? Shall I renew it again for next year?' They went a bit quiet, and then my dad said, 'Ah, do we have to? Can't we just go back to where we used to sit?' Truth be told, I think we were probably all happier just watching the match in a normal way and not having all the hassle of the other add-ons. We go for the match. If we get a cup of tea as well, that's a bonus.

So we got season tickets back in what is now named the Kenny Dalglish Stand, where we'd use to sit before I got famous. Before the first game of the new season, as we were walking up the stairs to our seats, Eddie asked me, 'Eh, John, are you sure you're going to be all right here? Because at least on the other side there were other celebs and stuff. Do you think people are going to be bothering you?' I said, 'No, nothing like that. People just aren't interested.' 'Well, we'll see,' he said.

We got to our seats and sat there, the three of us in a row. As soon as we sat down, a man behind us tapped me on the shoulder. As I turned around, he had a camera in his hand. I said, 'OK, that's fine, mate,' and I started to pose for him. He looked at me, baffled, and handed me the camera – he had come from Norway and he wanted me to take a picture of him and his mates.

I looked around me, and the great thing was that everybody sitting nearby had seen what had happened and were cracking up. It broke the ice for us sitting there and now going to the match is one of the places where people stop me the least for selfies. The reality is that any minor celebrity at a game is of no greater importance than anyone in the ground. The most important people are on the pitch and that is all anyone is really interested in.

I am lucky enough to be friends with people at the club like Peter Moore, the CEO, and Kenny Dalglish, who have both invited me to watch games in the boardroom rather than my usual seats. Last season they invited me to the Liverpool derby versus Everton. I took my dad for what turned out to be a really memorable day. When I arrived to pick my dad up, he was dressed as he would normally dress for the match – an ordinary shirt and a casual jacket. I was in smart trousers, a smart jacket and a tie.

'Have you got a tie?' I asked him.

'Why? Are we going to a wedding or a funeral on the way?' he said.

'No – it's just that we are in the boardroom, so I think you will need a tie.'

'It's a game of bloody football! Why will I need a tie?'

'Because ...'

I could tell my dad didn't want to go looking for a tie, and one thing I hope that I inherit from him as I get older is that look that says, 'I'm not wearing a tie, and if you make me, I am not going.'

'OK,' I said. 'Don't worry about it.'

We got in the car and drove to the ground. Liverpool's boardroom is in the impressive new main stand. As we filtered through the ground towards it, I could see that more and more people were wearing a tie. I didn't want my dad to feel self-conscious, especially as it was a situation that could make anyone feel nervous, knowing we were to have lunch with the CEO of the club we both love, along with one of the American owners.

As we approached the entrance to the boardroom, I was desperately trying to think of ways that I could resolve the situation, but I didn't have to. The staff were brilliant. Even though they knew who I was, they could tell this was a big day for both of us. My dad not having a tie made me feel even more like we didn't really belong there. Then, as I gave our names, one of the doormen turned to my dad and said: 'Mr Bishop, we have your tie here.'

Without making a fuss, they produced a tie and offered it to my dad, as if he had sent it ahead for them to have ready. His face had lost the 'I'm not wearing a tie and if you make me, I am not going!' look. Instead, he was as appreciative as I was and slipped the tie on, and we had a memorable afternoon that I will always treasure. Liverpool won with a bizarre last-minute goal from Divock Origi, and now my iPhone screensaver is a picture of me and Dad, in the players' tunnel, touching the famous 'This Is Anfield' sign.

This season that cross-generational joy continued when we took my six-year-old niece Eleanor to her first game. It was a home game against Newcastle, which we won 3–1. My sister Carol managed to capture the moment Sadio Mané scored on her phone, and the instant joy cascaded between me, my dad and Eleanor. There are decades between us but at that moment all three of us shared the same emotion. That is why football is so important, because not many things can do this. It can unite generations in families. It can give you a shared love of something. And it can also get my dad to wear a tie, which is no mean feat.

Playing for England

Watching football in your fifties compared to in your twenties might be a different world, but playing it is a different galaxy. I'll be playing five-a-side and will feel absolutely mortified when a rubbish player on the other team gets past me. I'll think, 'You wouldn't have got past me twenty years ago!' But then I realise that, in my fake memory, I'm thinking of myself as this person who should have been playing for England twenty years ago, as if I used to be Jamie Carragher. Whereas the truth is they would probably have got past me then, as well.

It's a sign of how big a part of my life football is that when I broke through with my comedy, a few years ago, and was able to buy a nice house in the countryside, the first thing that I did was to customise its tennis court. It had a tennis court, and I put five-a-side goals in to make it double up as a five-a-side football pitch. I added floodlights and then I got a dug-out. I'm not making this up: I got an actual dug-out. I was probably one step away from getting a stand and a commentary box and employing a referee and linesmen every time I played. I used to play five-a-side with my mates and a little voice in my head would be saying, 'I've made it – I've got my own dug-out in the garden!'

Part of getting old may be that you realise that you were never going to be a world-beating player, but I must admit it is annoying to see how my abilities have deteriorated. I have woken up after having dreams where I'm trying to play football and I literally can't move. I am on the pitch at Anfield, and I've got Jürgen Klopp shouting at me from the side. The ball is in front of me, and I can't move. I have had that dream a few times, and I always wake up and wonder if Jürgen has had a dream about shouting at a slightly overweight comedian who somehow has got on the pitch and can't move. What I have taken from the dream is that I am better watching than playing, because it's harder to let everyone down when you are only watching.

It makes me wonder if it's better to start a totally new sport in your fifties,* rather than just carry on playing something you've always played and watch yourself get worse at it. If you've never played golf before, or tennis, or badminton, the chances are that every time you play, you'll get a little bit better. Whereas if you carry on playing football, you'll just watch yourself get shitter and shitter and shitter.

Sometimes I watch myself get shitter in front of millions of people. I got involved just under ten years ago with the charity Soccer Aid, which meant that I found myself playing live on television, in front of millions of viewers as well as the 75,000 people inside Old Trafford. I was forty-three at the time, and I

---

* Maybe I should take up pole-vaulting! Watch out, Luke Cutts and Holly Bradshaw!

distinctly remember thinking, *If only I was still thirty-three, I'd be better than this. If I was still twenty-three, I'd be great!*

Even though this is a charity game for UNICEF, everyone taking part takes it seriously. It is obvious that the celebs would take it seriously because it is our chance to fulfil boyhood dreams, but I have always been surprised how serious some of the ex-players have taken it. In one Soccer Aid game, I was marking Andriy Shevchenko. He is the fifth top goal-scorer in history in all European competitions, with sixty-seven goals. He is the all-time top scorer for the Ukranian national team and has won league titles and cups in Italy with AC Milan, in England with Chelsea, and in Ukraine with Dynamo Kiev. He was awarded the highest honour for an individual footballer in 2004 when he received the Ballon d'Or.

Basically, I was forty-five and I was marking one of the best football players in the world. During the game, I was standing next to him when his team got a throw-in, and he leaned back into me and then threw himself to the ground. I couldn't believe it. He had dived in order to win a free kick, which the referee gave him. As he stood up, I said to him: 'For fuck's sake Andriy, mate, I'm a comedian. Why are you diving to get a free kick off me? *You're Andriy Shevchenko!*'

He just smiled and ran away and I have to admit that a big part of me likes that attitude – Andriy Shevchenko, diving to get a free kick off a middle-aged comedian in a charity match because he wants to win. I've got a similar mentality – I've always wanted to be good. I love having a little kickabout even now, when I've had corrective knee surgery. It limits how much I can play, but I still want to win.

I'm normally the oldest player on the pitch at every Soccer Aid unless Gordon Ramsay plays, who is three weeks older than me.

For the last one I took part in, Gordon wasn't there, so I was the oldest. Clive Tyldesley (cheers, Clive!) mentioned it in his TV commentary: 'John Bishop, one of the fittest forty-nine-year-olds you will see, and doing well for his age.' That comment says it all. Any comment that ends with 'for his age' basically means: we are all surprised he can actually move at all.

I have kept all the shirts from Soccer Aid because they are great memories, but I am not generally a mad football-shirt collector. As you get older, it is not quite so seemly to go to matches wearing your team's shirt. I will hold my hands up in that I've done it plenty of times in the past, but it is a young man's game. Thankfully, I never went as far as the Full-Kit Wanker look of sporting the shorts and socks as well. I think at *any* age, there is something severely lacking in your life if you are going to football matches dressed like that.

I have also never put my own name on the back of my Liverpool shirt. I don't know what the blokes who do that are thinking of. Well, maybe I do. As I've said on stage, I see fat guys in their kits at matches, with their name on the back, and I'm sure that a part of them is hoping that they'll turn up and Jürgen will look around and say, 'Jesus, I've just realised that we've only got ten players! Luckily, Fat Harry over there has got his own kit, let's put him in the team!'

I don't know if it's something about acknowledging your own age but I think as you head into middle age, you can get away with wearing retro kits more than the current team strip at games. The favourite retro kit that I own isn't even Liverpool. It's the retro Southport FC kit from the 1980s, when I was playing for them. It is long sleeved, golden in colour with black cuffs and collar, and it has the club crest on it along with the sponsor's logo Apollo Leisure on the front. It is made from the type of polyester that you no longer see, the type that has a pattern ingrained into it so that it shimmers under light, which did help when you were covered in mud from some pitch in the North of England – but I thought it was great when I first wore it and I think the same now. A friend from Southport bought it for me as a fiftieth birthday present and I love it. It's brilliant because it means nothing at all to anybody but me.

When I was a lad, buying a programme was part of the whole match-day experience. It seemed important. I'd read it cover-to-cover and it was the only way to find out what the manager was thinking and what the captain was saying. Nowadays, of course, I realise that I can just as easily listen to them saying the same things on Sky, and the official programme is really just glossy, overpriced club PR stuff.

Yet the weird thing is that when I go to the games, I still buy them. The programmes used to be like the Bible, and nowadays, for me, they're more like the Bible in that *maybe I'll get around to reading them one day*. They just lie around at home, until Melanie tells me to chuck them out: 'John, I can understand you keeping Cup Final programmes, but why have you got one here for a midweek game against Derby County in the Carabao Cup, three years ago?' And I haven't got an answer.

My love of football has led me to presenting a new show on Amazon Prime called *Back of the Net* with Gabby Logan and Peter Crouch. It's a weekly show about the Premier League and, at the time of writing, we are just about to start filming it, so hopefully when you read this it is still on. I say that because I can not, as a football supporter, think of any better job than to make a show based on the weekend's football. I can now even claim that I am working when I am sat on my backside watching the football.

If I try to explain how my relationship with football has changed as I've got older, I'd say it's that now I massively appreciate how good and how dedicated anybody who makes it as a footballer, or in any sport, must be. Like any father who has sons, I have gone through the stage of thinking, I'm going to make you be a footballer! The truth is, you might as well think, I'm going to make you be a skydiver! They may have all the skill in the world, but they've also got to have some luck and single-minded commitment.

I've talked in my stand-up about how much football has changed in my lifetime. I used to say that you used to go and watch football and everyone in the ground was four steps away from somebody on the pitch. They were local lads. Everyone knew someone who knew someone who knew someone who knew someone who was playing. Nowadays the players might as well have been dropped in from outer space. Sadio Mané and Roberto Firmino are fantastic footballers but nobody in Anfield went to school with them, or went out with their sister, or played against them for the school team. They arrive without any shared history, which is inevitable but a shame.

Despite that, I think Liverpool FC feels a bit more connected to the city than it has done for years and years. A lot of it is down to Jürgen Klopp, and to the success, but that's not the whole story. People will complain about the money the players earn, and you can see their point, but at the same time there's a vague socialist element to it. It's not the complete vision of Karl Marx because the workers don't own the means of production but, even so, it's still the workers getting the bulk of the money. It's not the players' fault that Rupert Murdoch or somebody wants to pay a billion pounds for the television rights. There is something that feels appropriate within football, in that the players receive the bulk of the money. It could be held up as an example of meritocracy, where those that are the best at the skill defined as the most important within that sphere receive the majority of the rewards. Yet despite this, or because of it, it is a disgrace that not all the Premier League clubs pay the living wage to their ancillary staff. It's simply not excusable.

Maybe as I grow older I can see the big picture more, but I think football as a form of entertainment is astounding. To get millions of eyeballs on something two or three times per week, and get 60,000 people paying to watch them every weekend – if any rock band in the world was doing that, it would be phenomenal. And the funny thing is, at least with the band, you'd know the gig would be great. There is no concert equivalent to a nil–nil bore-draw on a cold winter's night when you spend the whole game thinking, *I've given half of my day up to watch this shite!*

Horses for Courses

The other sport we'd occasionally get into in my household when I was a kid was horse racing. When I was a boy it was a tradition in our house, like in houses all over the country, to all choose horses for the Grand National at Aintree, and Dad would place the bets on our behalf. In 1974, when I was seven, I even managed to pick Red Rum as the winner.

I have fond memories of the Grand National, but in recent years, as I have become more committed to animal welfare, I have grown increasingly uncomfortable about an event that every year results in the deaths of horses. Some people will argue that the horses are bred for the event and have incredible lives, receiving the best of everything, and that as the Grand National is such a prestigious event the risk is worth the reward. I will accept this argument the day someone shows me a horse entering itself into the race.

I don't object to horse racing per se, and I have enjoyed days at places like Chester races where there are no jumps. It just seems to me that horses would not naturally go around jumping over fences but if we are to ask them to do this there is no need to make the jumps so difficult that they become dangerous. During the three-day National meeting, an average of three horses die each year. I just don't think it's acceptable that any animal should lose its life in pursuit of entertainment, which is also why I believe all blood sports should be banned. I understand some animals need to be culled to manage the countryside, and I have seen the damage foxes can do when they get into chicken coops, but the cull shouldn't be sport or entertainment. People shouldn't kill any living beings for pleasure. I think we will come to look back on such practices – as we do with the gladiators of the Roman Empire – as an illustration of the dark side of humanity.

A few years ago, a mate of mine contacted me to ask if I could host a press event to launch the Grand National weekend. He already knew of my misgivings about the event so he had told the organisers that I would probably say no, which I did. The organisers asked if I might instead do a voiceover introducing the event and the individual speakers on the stage. I explained that I would feel uncomfortable doing even this, and jokingly suggested that my friend should instead phone my brother, Eddie. Eddie has exactly the same voice as me and I knew that nobody would be able to tell the difference. It worked: he phoned Eddie, Eddie did the voiceover, and nobody was any the wiser.

At the time I thought this was funny, but looking back now I can see that it made it look as if I am a supporter of the Grand National. Though I applaud what it does for the Liverpool economy, I think it can do more to enhance horse safety. I know it has made efforts in this area, but I think more can be done. Formula One enhanced its safety measures and didn't put any fans off; I'm sure that would be the same with the Grand National. And thus I can't call myself a supporter. I have loads of friends who go every year and enjoy it; I think people have to make their own choice but it's not for me. Maybe one major consequence of growing older, and nearer to the end of my own life, is that I value the life of everything a little more than I used to. And that includes horses.

I am not entirely against horse racing itself. I even had a share in a horse syndicate with a few mates. We had a horse call Know My Name, which ran on the flat and did quite well, but we had to retire it because it developed a form of hay fever. If there is anything that suggests you do not belong in horse racing it is having a stake in a horse that develops hay fever. I am glad to say that the horse is now enjoying its retirement in a field somewhere, no doubt receiving a horse dose of antihistamine.

Men and Supermen

When I think about sport nowadays, I come back to that difference between mortals like me and what the very top professional sportsmen can do. I have more appreciation now of how good another human being can be at what they do, especially when you have lived enough to know the distance between them and you.

I think it would make for a great TV programme. I should have a race with Usain Bolt to show just how fast he is. We only ever see Usain Bolt running against other people who can run the 100 metres in ten seconds – what if you saw him running against an ordinary person like me, who'd probably come in after he has done a lap of honour, had a shower and gone home? Then we would know how good he is (and how average I am, which is why I have not actually pushed the idea too far!).

I did a similar thing a few years ago when I went cycling with a few mates in France. It's possible to follow the Tour de France course: you go to the course and a few hours before the racers begin, you can cycle on the route because they are essentially ordinary roads. It's good because the crowds are already starting to assemble for the race, so you have an audience. We were going over the mountains and the crowds were shouting to encourage us: *'Oui, oui! Allez! Allez!'* There were some fellas who had got off their bikes and were just walking, but we gave it our best shot.

An hour or so later they closed the road and the Tour de France proper came through. I have never felt so diminished in my life. I had put everything I had into riding that bit of course, but when I watched the racers speed past, they looked like an optical illusion. They were genuinely going up the hill faster than I had gone down the other side of it. It was just absolutely phenomenal.

Increasing numbers of middle-aged men are taking up cycling, a sport where being a Full-Kit Wanker is actively encouraged, even if that kit looks like it is trying to hold back your body from exploding all over the road. Cycling has created the phenomenon of the MAMIL – Middle-Aged Men In Lycra – because it's enjoyable, it's accessible and it's easy to take up. All you need to know is how to ride a bike. You wouldn't get far turning up with a full Lycra kits, helmet, shades and a £5,000 bike ... on stabilisers.

The other week, I did some mountain biking around where I am currently living, in Sussex. I went with a mate, John, who is working on my house, and another friend of ours, Jim, who works as a builder with John and is a very fit sixty-one-year-old. We biked along all the trails and it was fantastic but part of me thought that if somebody had told me, when I was twenty, that in my fifties I'd go mountain-bike riding with another mate in his fifties, and somebody in his sixties, I'd have thought they were taking the piss. Especially if they also said that the bloke in his sixties would win the race at the end.

My dad, in his fifties, would never have done something like go mountain biking with his mates. It comes down to the fact that my generation is the one that still expects to be physical and to be playing sport in middle age – *carpe diem*, and all that. The only problem comes when you physically can't do it anymore.

Fat Back Banned

That's the whole challenge – staying healthy and staying fit as you grow older. It's not easy. As you age, one particular saying grows ever truer: *A minute on the lips and a month on the hips.* Last week I was putting some jeans on in front of a mirror and looking at myself. I shook myself and everything wobbled. Everything. Even my back wobbled. I didn't know back fat was a thing. I don't know what you eat that decides to settle on your *back*, but once you see it, it can't be unseen. I am now convinced that the only way I will now ever look proportionally right is if I grow another foot taller.

In your twenties, you never get fat. Or if you do, you must have tried really hard. You can eat anything, do anything and you don't put any weight on. Those days are long gone now for me. It does at least help me that I've been vegetarian since I was eighteen, so I'm not eating meat and two veg, or wolfing down kebab and chips late at night. I'm trying to be as vegan as I can now, because as I get older, I find I feel better without dairy, and it is not good for my throat when I'm on tour, in addition to all the ethical reasons behind not eating diary. But even with all that, I still have to work hard just to stay still and not give in to middle-aged spread.

I tried having a personal trainer but it didn't really work for me. I couldn't get into it. They'd say, 'Right, pick that weight up and do twelve repetitions!' Then they would just watch me and count: 'One ... two ... three ... right, that's twelve, you can stop!' I would think, *I could have done that myself.* I was basically just paying people to count.

I also do some pad work with a trainer where I pretend I could have been a boxer. This is clearly not the case, because in all the sessions I have had with him, he has never once hit me back. As he used to be a cage fighter, I think if he *did* hit me back, I would have to start paying someone to count again.

What works best for me is going to the gym. I go on my own, early in the morning. When I wake up, I *never* want to go, but after I have gone to the gym, I am at least a 50 per cent better human being. I can think more. I'm more efficient. I get up at five or six in the morning and do gym training or a spin class. It's cathartic for me. Some people need transcendental meditation, and some people need a twenty-five-year-old woman in Lycra yelling at them to pedal faster. We all have to locate our own inner karma.

That's one strange thing that age does to you. You grow to like early mornings. I don't sleep as much as I used to nowadays. I don't go to bed so late and I go to bed sober more often than not. I've got a clear head, am raring to go, and it's great. I love being awake when nobody else is. There is something a bit vampire-ish about it: that five-in-the-morning feeling when there's no one about and it feels a bit like being around in the world after a virus has killed everyone. It's quiet and calm and I answer all my emails and get stuff done. It's the time of day I do my best work nowadays. Mind you, I need an afternoon nap to make up for it!

There again, going to the gym is a generational thing as well, and to do with the life that I lead. In the same way that he never went mountain biking, my dad never went to the gym. He worked on building sites: you don't work on a building site all day and then go, 'I think I need to work on my quads tonight. I need to isolate my glutes.' My dad and his mates didn't need to do that because they spent the day grafting. I just ponce around on a stage, talking.

Even doing that, I have to look after myself. As well as my own general sense of wellbeing, there is a professional element as to why I need to keep myself fit in middle age. You lose muscle mass as you get older. When I'm on stage, in order to have presence and speak and project properly, I need to have proper stature. If I start to slump and stand badly, it will affect my voice. Training properly can actually extend my career.

Nobody in my line of work used to think like that. A lot of the big TV comedians used to be out of shape, probably because they'd had five pints before they went on stage. But today is a different environment and a different expectation. It comes down to the fact that for a lot of people, the aesthetics matter as much as the content, or even more. If you look good, people will buy into you. If you don't, they're not interested.

Touring is good for me because I have a focus and I try to look after myself as much as I can. I never drink before a gig. I might occasionally have a drink on a night off or I might have a drink after a gig if I have a day off the next day, but as the Mayo Clinic has told us, one of the best things you can do as you get older is drink less alcohol. I certainly drink less when I am on the road.

As you get older, your relationship with your body changes and you suffer all sorts of indignities. I used to do a stand-up routine about going for a prostate check, because it is the weirdest experience. I talked about how I went to see this doctor and I was expecting him to put on rubber gloves, but instead he put on a single-finger rubber, like a condom for his finger. He had me on all fours, and he had his finger up my bum. He wasn't saying anything, so – and I don't know what I was thinking – I said: 'Are you busy?'

I mean, he's a GP, of course he's busy! I was behaving like I was in the hairdresser's. I was trying to break the ice with somebody who had his finger up my arse. That is one moment when you really don't have to break the ice. The ice has already been shattered.

But I kept going. I actually asked him, 'What are you looking for?'

'I'm just trying to feel around for something,' he told me. 'It feels a little bit like a Brussel sprout.'

I suppose the worst thing that you could do is go for a prostate examination on Boxing Day. There is a good chance you would get a false positive result.

I've learned to accept, or at least work around, the inconveniences of my body getting older – the bad backs, and all that. I wake up in the morning feeling like a Picasso painting, with none of my bits hanging together properly, but a good spin class soon puts that right.

Starting the day right is vital. I find if I am limping by the time that I leave the house, I will limp all day, even if I don't know why I am limping. I keep thinking of getting into yoga or Pilates, something that is supposed to stretch you out.

Another option is tai chi. I came across tai chi this year when I was making a TV programme for ITV about moving two beluga whales from Shanghai to a sanctuary in Iceland. This was a brilliant experience and it was a world first, as nobody had ever previously tried to set up a sanctuary for beluga whales that had been held in captivity. It involved incredible logistics as the whales had to be lifted through the window of their aquarium, placed in a purpose-built steel container, lifted onto an articulated lorry and driven to Shanghai Airport to be flown to Reykjavik. There, they were lifted onto another lorry and driven across Iceland and onto a ferry to the sanctuary on the island of Heimaey.

Now, most people might suspect that the journey alone would be enough for a TV documentary. However, the director felt that we needed to establish that I was 'actually in China' so he organised for me to do some tai chi, the slow-motion martial art. I thought it was a stupid idea but I did it anyway and it was absolutely brilliant.

I went to a local park and joined a group of people in their seventies who were amazing in their poise and strength. Afterwards, I was totally knackered. Talking to them, it was clear that they put tai chi central to their life and wellbeing and that it kept them fit physically and mentally. Shanghai's parks were full of older people doing it. I was so impressed that I promised myself I would take it up after I got home. I have put it on my list, just below learning to play that piano.

Golf

The real sporting cliché for middle-aged men is taking up golf. The main issue for me there is that I have always considered it a complete waste of time. However, I recently played at a corporate event, having not picked up golf clubs for at least three years, and I thoroughly enjoyed it.

It's another rite of passage of aging: I have now become old enough to think that golf might be OK. Over the years, I have been invited to various golf events and I've always approached them in the same way: that I will enjoy the two or three shots that I hit well and, though I will be rubbish for the rest of the day, will enjoy the walk anyway. It's a paradox: there is no more micro-managed and manicured piece of countryside than a golf course, and yet you can walk off the course and pretend to yourself that you have engaged with nature.

The problem I have with golf is that I have never been bothered that I am no good at it. This seems to annoy other people when you play with them. More than once I have been the 'celebrity' member of a golf team at charity or corporate events. Each time, I have seen how disappointed my teammates are when they see my first tee shot and realise that I am rubbish, when they could have had a good golfer like James Nesbitt or just about any footballer. They have often paid thousands of pounds from company funds to sponsor the event and play a round of golf with a celeb. They may be quietly hoping that they might win a prize in the team competition, or at very least enjoy a round of golf with an interested partner. Instead they get a comedian who is rubbish and who looks bored after seven holes.

Golf just goes on for too long. It is the last bastion of the imperial measures system. No other sport operates within the dozen-

and-a-half framework. There is no other reason that a golf course has to be eighteen holes, except that a dozen seemed not enough and two dozen was too many for the middle-aged Scottish people who invented the game.

People have used sticks to hit balls for centuries but it is the Scots who are credited with developing the modern sport of golf. Their passion for the game was such that, in 1457, King James II of Scotland banned it because it was distracting the men of the country from practising archery, which he saw as a more useful activity when it came to defending the country from invasion. He was probably right: an arrow fired at the heart is always going to deter invaders more than a ball flying through the air as your foe tries to catch you unawares by not shouting 'FORE!'

There is no more middle-aged sport than golf, and as you get older you are fairly likely to embrace it. However, there are a number of glaring things wrong with the sport:

1. The clothing.
2. It takes too long. Spending four to five hours doing *anything* is a big commitment, especially when it comes to hitting a small ball and walking after it.
3. Many people who play golf are wankers. Now, there is a percentage of wankers in all walks of life, and certainly not everyone who plays golf is a wanker. However, I think we have to accept that it is a sport where there is a higher percentage of wankers than is normal. Any sport where it is acceptable to have someone else carry your bag is likely to attract wankers, and there are some golf courses where a caddy is actually compulsory. You cannot play the course unless someone else carries your bag, and in some places, caddies are not permit-

ted to use trollies but have to physically carry the bags. These courses are wanker magnets.

4. It's really, really difficult. If you want to make people enjoy your sport, make the holes bigger, the courses shorter, and instead of having caddies, have a man who stands in the bunker and throws you your ball back every time it goes in it.

Let's Face the Music

I am still not sure golf will be my sport for my older years. In fact, I think I have found another one: dancing. Dancing appears to be the activity that has the biggest impact on dementia according to a study that I recently read by the Albert Einstein College of Medicine in New York City, and published in the *New England Journal of Medicine*.

Conducted over a period of twenty-one years, the study looked at senior citizens of seventy-five years and older. The researchers measured mental acuity in aging by monitoring rates of dementia. The aim of the study was to find out if any physical or cognitive recreational activities had an effect on mental acuity – in other words, is it better to join a pub quiz or go for a run?

The study found that some cognitive activities influence mental acuity, but almost none of the physical activities had any effect. The one exception was frequent dancing. Some findings of the studies were:

- Reading – 35 per cent reduced risk of dementia
- Bicycling and swimming – 0 per cent reduced risk of dementia

- Doing crossword puzzles at least four days a week – 47 per cent reduced risk of dementia
- Playing golf – 0 per cent reduced risk of dementia
- Dancing frequently – 76 per cent reduced risk of dementia

It emerged that people who dance regularly have greater cognitive reserves and an increased complexity of neuronal synapses. Dancing lowered the risk of dementia by improving these neural qualities. It may cause the brain to continually rewire its neural pathways because it is filled with quick movements and you have to constantly reassess what you are doing and what your partner is doing. You need spatial awareness, and you need to communicate with others. Along with engaging with the music it appears the combination stimulates the brain and helps to reduce dementia.

I am a long way from appearing on *Strictly Come Dancing*, but who knows? Maybe dancing should be my new way of staying fit and alert as I grow older. There may well soon be a dance class somewhere with a new member. Though I would imagine I will be the only dancer wearing a retro 1980s Southport Town FC shirt.

8.
HOW TO STAY RELEVANT

AS I HEAD DEEP into middle age, I find it increasingly harder to keep up with the cutting edge in culture or technology. It comes down to this basic fact: *I've got unlimited access to a world that I can't understand and I can't use.*

This ignorance is partly because I can't be arsed with keeping up, but also because the cutting edge in culture and technology keeps on changing. By the time I have sussed what is going on, the cutting edge in culture and technology has pissed off somewhere else entirely. It's started doing something else, and I've got a whole load of new stuff to try and learn.

When it comes to technology, I would guess I use 10 per cent of the capacity of everything I own. I don't know how anything works, and just as I'm learning and beginning to feel that I am part of the Silicon Valley New Age, someone invents something else. What we really need is a year where nobody is allowed to invent anything. Nobody is allowed to come up with a new thing and we are all allowed to find out how everything we own works. There should be a United Nations memorandum sent around the globe, stating: *'This year is a catch-up year. Everybody is allowed to catch up with their stuff and learn what it does. If you have a good idea during this year, write it down and wait – anyone found inventing anything will be sent to jail until the year is over.'*

Without such a moratorium, I feel I am forever in a race with technology that I am never going to win because someone keeps moving the finish line. At my age, I am firmly part of the generation who were amazed and amused to find that '80085', when typed into the new things that kids had started bringing to school called pocket calculators, spelled 'BOOBS'. For a teenage boy who was increasingly fascinated by this particular subject, this was a brilliant validation that the subject merited further study – why, even new electronic devices were interested in boobs!

The world has moved on. Nowadays, if I type the word 'boobs' into Google on my computer, there are roughly a trillion images, articles and videos that I simply will not live long enough to study. Boobs are just an example of how much information is out there. It is far too much to possibly take in, which means that I'm floundering trying to keep up with the pace of modern life, and so I have taken the decision not to bother. I have no idea what is Number One in the pop chart (mind you, that has been the case for about thirty years) and in terms of being trendy or relevant, I am years behind on the latest films or musical trends.

I am absolutely fine with this state of affairs because I don't want to go chasing something that is not for me. I am in my fifties, and if someone aged nineteen is breaking into the charts and singing a song for me, they are making a big mistake because I'm not listening. I'm listening to country and western, and some bloke who's telling me a story about his horse dying and his wife leaving and how his dog has got a limp. That's my world. I don't need the optimism of a nineteen-year-old telling me how many people he slept with this week in my life.

Not everybody shares my view. I've got mates who work in the music business and every time I see them, they're a little bit cooler and they've got a little bit more hair dye and their clothes are a little bit edgier. That's not for me. I feel like saying to them, 'Come on lads, you're in your forties – you're dressing younger than the bands you're trying to sign!' But I don't, because I'd like to hang on to at least a few cool mates. However, when I've made the comment about hair dye, I can imagine thought bubbles above the heads of one or two of them: *Does that knob mean me? I thought nobody could tell!*

Social media develops at lightning speed. The first time someone came up to me and said, 'Can I have a Snapchat?' I had absolutely no idea what they were talking about. I genuinely wondered if they were asking me for some kind of bread-based snack.

I know now that Snapchat is where somebody takes a photo or a video, sends it to someone and it's visible to them for a few seconds before it disappears into some kind of cyber-space rubbish bin. It's supposed to vanish into the ether. But it doesn't always disappear. People can find a way to hold on to it, share it with others or use it against you, which is where a lot of cyber-porn blackmail comes from. We have moved from a world where someone would try to shame an ex-partner by writing 'Tracy is a slag' on the toilet wall in school to today, when sex tapes are posted all over the internet for the world to see.

The fragile nature of relationships, as people move from virginity through their teenage years to early adulthood, is now a minefield where the journey from first base to home run has been replaced by a swipe right on a dating app in the morning and a sex tape in the afternoon. The majority of victims of sex-tape blackmail are women, as more young men coerce their new partners into engaging in something for 'fun', which can be used against them later.

Snapchat is also a potential explanation for the phenomenon of the dick pic. This is where a man has decided to send a partner, or a potential partner, a picture of his penis as an illustration of the fun that may be set to follow. There are millions of dick pics flying around the globe in cyberspace because young men think they will go no further. This is not always the case, and it shows how the progress of human development is not always linear. One step forward can lead to one step back.

Just think about it. We are able to do wonderful things with the internet and computer technology, and what some men have chosen to do with it in 2019 is to use it to send photos of their genitals to other people. Male genitals are not even aesthetically pleasing. Even God couldn't be bothered to put any effort in. He used whatever was lying around in His animal-kingdom workshop, which is why we ended up with something that looks like it was made from leftover turkey necks, quails' eggs and a gorilla's finger, all framed in badger hair. I think it's fair to say that if you wake up in the morning, look down at that part of your body and think *I bet so-and-so would love a look at this right now*, you are truly deluded enough to deserve it popping up on your mum's Facebook page.

Grimewatch

Trying to remain up-to-date in a world where up-to-date moves on by the minute is just too much effort. I watched Stormzy headline Glastonbury this summer and I watched it at home, in my study, drinking tea. There can hardly be a greater contrast than a white, middle-aged man in his house tracksuit/lounge pants, sat in his spare room that he calls a study, watching the biggest musical event in the country on Catch Up (because he is so out of tune that not only does he not go to the event, he doesn't even watch it live).

I watched the first British black solo-artist to headline at Glastonbury take to the stage, play urban-based grime music and perform one of the most legendary sets ever performed at the event ... from my spare room. I didn't feel too bad about this because every time the camera panned across the crowd, it seemed to contain mostly other middle-class white people like me, who appreciate Stormzy's music and his message but cannot pretend to have lived his life. It was a bold booking and it will shift the landscape in terms of the voices represented at Glastonbury. This would not be a bad thing because, at times, there looked to be more black people on the stage than there were in the crowd – and there were 100,000 people in the crowd.

There is no question that Stormzy smashed it. He smashed it in every way – the artistry, the forcefulness of his message, the choreography of the ballet, the other contributors who joined him on stage, the symbolism of the stab vest he wore with the Banksy Union Jack on the front and the roll call of the grime artists who had paved the way for him and those to follow. All of it hit home. The performance had energy, purpose and power. And despite me being a million miles away from being the target audience for grime, I loved every minute of it as I sat in my study, drinking tea and eating toast.

In the past, I would have wished I was there at Glastonbury. I would have been kicking myself for missing the opportunity to see something special. I would been annoyed that I was missing out on the kudos and coolness of being able to say (along with 99,999 other people): *'Yeah, I was there. I mean, I know you can get a really good view and hear everything on the TV but, really, you have to be there – in a farmer's field, squashed up with thousands of people you don't know, a mile away from the stage, behind an LGBT flag that means you can't see a thing but which you can't ask to be taken down in case you appear homophobic. Yeah, you had to be there!'*

Well, this year I was content to watch Glastonbury at home. I missed a significant moment in the festival's history but I was watching it in fresh, clean clothes, sober, shaved, refreshed, suffering neither heatstroke nor pneumonia, and within thirty seconds of the nearest toilet. As you hit middle age, all of this stuff is increasingly vital.

Melanie and I came late to the world of festivals. We went to our first Glastonbury in 2011, when I was already forty-four. At an age when people decide to take up golf, or pottery, we went to our first rock festival. We were complete novices but it was something I had always wanted to do so I paid a stupid amount of money to stay in a Winnebago on a farm next door to the event. We went without any kids: this was to be something for us, and the last thing we needed was the distraction of teenagers to look after.*

That 2011 Glastonbury was my gift to Melanie, a veritable feast of music for us to gorge on and to reinvigorate our relationship with live music. But our ignorance about how Glaston-

---

* *Well, that is what we told ourselves. The reality was that I did not want my lack of festival coolness to be further emphasised by me constantly asking my kids to stay close to me so that I could ask them who all the cool bands were, and if I was standing next to a pop star.*

bury worked was ridiculous. Melanie had gone through the programme for the whole festival and marked down what she wanted to see, like an aunty with the TV guide at Christmas. She'd say, 'We'll be fine, there are ten minutes between these two acts,' but then we found that also between the two acts were a mile and a half, 100,000 drunk and/or stoned people, and a swamp. Basically, at Glastonbury, where you start the afternoon is where you finish it.

Staying in a Winnebago, we missed the 'real' Glastonbury experience, and thank God for that. I have never woken up in a tent next to people I don't know, having not washed for three days. I have never become so used to using a fetid long-drop toilet that I have begun to have doubts about flushing toilets because someone called Horse, who I met at the cider bus, convinced me that flushing toilets were destroying the world because evil corporate interests would rather use water to clean away the shit of the west than feed the crops of Africa.*

We slept in a hired Winnebago and not in a tent the first time we went to Glastonbury because, as festival virgins, I wanted our experience to be as hassle-free as possible. To be fair, we have never been a camping family, and if we were to start I would rather it be in a sanctioned holiday park in Wales with decent amenities and a camp shop – not a field in Somerset three inches away from the next tent, among thousands of drunk people, in very real danger of being pissed on in the night by someone who was lost and just had to go.

---

* *Those are the type of conversations that you have at Glastonbury. I know because I have had them. I have never slept in a tent there but I did meet a man called Horse at the cider bus.*

I tried to write off the cost of the Winnebago but I have to be honest – by the second night, when I was doing the seventy-five-minute walk to what was effectively a posh caravan, next to a load of other posh caravans, which was costing us more that it would cost to actually buy a posh caravan, I was becoming slightly disillusioned with our first Glastonbury. However, our weekend was saved by bumping into Chris Moyles. That is not a sentence I ever expected to write but it was certainly true, because Chris and his friends made our Glastonbury experience brilliant.

We were sat in what was called a VIP area but this must come with a caveat. Glastonbury, for all of its utopian ideals, does have a genuine hierarchy. In some respects, this is understandable. There are 135,000 people at the festival, many of them not behaving in the most inhibited way, and there are also some of the biggest names in music and entertainment. If ever there was a rationale for a VIP area, being in a field surrounded by the uninhibited and chemically altered is one of them.

Between the Pyramid Stage and the Other Stage at Glastonbury is one big VIP area which has a huge bar, food stalls and – most importantly – toilets. It's a step up from the mayhem and queues outside with the rest of the attendees, but you are not in the most exclusive area that holds the celebs who end up being photographed at Glastonbury. There is always the feeling that there is another more exclusive place. That is because *there is*, and you can almost see it behind the fencing at the side of the VIP area.

This wire fencing is the equivalent of the rope outside a local nightclub. You are either on the good side of it or you are not. Not being on the good side of it makes you believe that, over there, people will be having a much better time than you. In fact, they will be slimmer, wealthier, sexier and happier than you will ever be ... unless you are allowed to join them, in which case, you will immediately be elevated to the same status of perfection. Well, 'slim and sexy' are not descriptions I would normally apply to me or Chris Moyles, but when he produced two passes for this VVIP promised land for me and Melanie, that is exactly what we all became.

Once you get into a VVIP area at Glastonbury, you can meet anybody and everybody. I knew things had gone to another level when I was backstage at a subsequent festival and found myself standing at a bar waiting for a drink next to Johnny Depp. I was slightly thrown but I managed to keep my cool long enough to say 'All right, Johnny!' as I walked away. I'm not 100 per cent sure that he replied but over that weekend, I convinced myself that I'd heard him say, 'Hey man, I love your work ...'

These are the areas of VIP access that no money would get you in. They are purely by invitation and you only get that invitation if you are one of the acts, high up in the music industry, or you are very famous. In the first year we hung around the 'standard' VIP area until we met Chris, but in the subsequent years I have managed to spend time in the more restricted VVIP and VVVIP areas, due to having some mates who are high up in the music industry.

It may be a shameful confession, but I have to admit that, despite the fact they essentially offer little more than a place to sit and access to a bar, it inflates your self-esteem to know that you are allowed in somewhere very few people can go. It's pathetic and definitely not in the festival spirit but I love it. The Holy Grail is the inner sanctums where the wrist bands and lanyards required to gain access are like gold dust. Basically, you have to be Bono, and even he can't get his mates in.

Bursting Our Bublé

Melanie used to love going to music gigs and I would willingly go to watch anyone she recommended. Then the kids came along and we started going ... nowhere. But after Glastonbury gave us our mojo (or our *Mojo* ... see what I did there?) back, we have been to loads of great things, from people breaking through like Miles Kane and Jack Savoretti to legends such as Elton John and U2. Now we are blessed with being able to see things from privileged vantage points, such as watching Elton from the side of the stage in Brighton just this year.

We often choose to see acts we really like outside of the UK because it all adds to the excitement of the experience. The first time we did it was for Michael Bublé in Paris in 2010. It was a treat for Melanie as she has always liked him so I pushed the boat out and organised a nice hotel, first-class tickets on Eurostar, and great seats. We made our way to the Bercy Arena and sat watching the support act in anticipation of Michael coming on.

The curtain closed. After a few minutes of inaction a man in a suit stood on the stage and Michael Bublé came out and stood next to him. There was some applause as a few people assumed this was the (rather low-key) start to the show. Then Michael Bublé began talking, and after each sentence he paused as the man in the suit translated what he had said into French. Michael explained that his very close friend, and drummer in the band, had been taken ill that afternoon and had had to go to hospital. As he was a key member of the band, Michael felt that he could not carry on and do the show without him, so he apologised but the show that night was cancelled.

I sat and listened with Melanie, having travelled on the train to London, then Paris on the Eurostar, then dropped our bags at a hotel to rush to the concert only to be told that it was cancelled by the very man we came to see. Before I could even work out what I made of that, it became apparent there was a cultural divide within the audience. The French seemed to greet the news with understanding and empathy. Nods of understanding and even a ripple of applause greeted Michael saying he would have to pull the show.

From what I could tell, the few English people in the crowd were slightly more miffed and less empathetic. I genuinely heard a man near to us, talking to himself but probably summarising what all the Brits were thinking, say: 'For fuck's sake, Bublé, he's a drummer! There are loads of drummers, just get another one! There are even machines that drum. I mean, how fucking ill is the bloke? Def Leppard have got a drummer who's only got one arm!'

That disappointment has not stopped us enjoying other jaunts to Europe to watch artists we like. Last year, that effort was rewarded in spectacular fashion when we went to see U2 in Milan. I love U2 and I have seen them live more than anyone else. Prior to this particular gig, I had already seen them live in the UK, Ireland, America and France. I have been lucky enough to have met the band, and have become friendly with the drummer, Larry Mullen Jr.

At the Milan gig, Larry's assistant greeted us as we arrived at the gig and told us that she would come to get us at the end so we could make a quick getaway. She was true to her word: at the start of the final song we were led to the back of the venue, where there was a fleet of twenty identical Mercedes people carriers. We were led to one and climbed inside, to be joined by a few other friends of the band.

We sat there for ten minutes while I wondered what we had gained by leaving before the last song to sit in a car and not go anywhere. Then it became apparent that we had been waiting for the show to end, and the band to get into the cars. All of a sudden we were off, a twenty-car cavalcade being led through the streets of Milan by a police escort.

I had never been involved in anything like it before. There was a unique excitement in looking out of the car window to see police motorbike outriders stopping the traffic to allow the convoy through without delay or hindrance. They weren't just police officers on motorbikes but *Italian* police officers on motorbikes, and therefore the coolest looking of all police officers on motorbikes. I tried to pretend it was all no big deal, but inside I was thinking, *I wish my mates could see me now! Or if not my mates, somebody else's mates! Anyone! Because I will never again be as cool as I am right now!*

We arrived at the hotel. As the band got out of their people carriers and Melanie and I got out of ours, there was a man in a smart Savile Row type suit coming out of the hotel front door. He spotted me and wandered over, completely missing one of the world's biggest rock bands right next to him. In a cut-glass posh Home Counties accent, he said, 'Oh, my Lord! What a surprise!' I imagined that he must be a journalist and prepared to say 'No comment' and head into the hotel. But instead, the posh bloke said this: 'I really can't *believe* this! I saw you at the train station last week. If you recall, it was the train from Waterloo, and I was getting onto my scooter, and you said something about it being a jolly good idea having a scooter instead of having to wait for a taxi. Bugger me! What a small world!'

I had just arrived in a cavalcade of people carriers escorted by Italian police officers on motorbikes. Screaming U2 fans were being held back by security, blue lights were flashing, the biggest rock band in the world and their entourage, of which we were temporarily part, were being led into the hotel next to us ... and the guy never acknowledged any of it. He just wanted to share that he had bumped into me at a train station the week before. I was desperate to be spotted, and when I was, it was by someone who couldn't give a toss how cool I thought I was.

One great thing about music is that, as you grow older, it can actually mean more to you that it did when you were younger – sometimes more than you even know yourself. Melanie and I went to see the Electric Light Orchestra at the O2 last year. Melanie's parents always played their music so she knew them from her childhood, and I am always up for going to see anyone live. As I had played the O2 only the year before, we managed to get tickets in a box.

This can be awkward because you are trapped with people that you don't know, but because it was short notice, we just appreciated whatever tickets we could get. In any case, we had no need to worry about being trapped with people we did not know as we arrived to find that we were the only ones there, with a whole range of canapés and drinks to enjoy as we watched ELO. Result!

I relaxed in my seat and began to tap my foot as I recognised songs that had peppered my childhood. Then, suddenly, they started playing 'Wild West Hero' and I burst into tears. I just couldn't stop. It powerfully reminded me of wanting to be a cowboy as a kid, of loving the song and the video so much, of how hopeful and optimistic it used to make me feel, and it just got to me. Melanie asked me what was wrong and I couldn't explain it to her.*

I have had moments like this in recent years, as I grow older: moments where a memory or a thought takes me back to my childhood. More often than not, it makes me smile, but sometimes it overwhelms me because for a second I can see the world through those eyes again, and I want to tell my naïve, younger self: 'Don't worry. It will be OK. You will find yourself in places you never imagined and you will have experiences you cannot even dream of now. You won't be a cowboy, but you will come close.'

I think that is true. In the world of showbusiness comedians are like cowboys. We ride into town alone, do what we have got to do, and ride out alone. We don't have gun fights, look good in Stetsons, camp out under the stars or drive cattle across the range, and most of us don't die with our boots on, but the life I have now is as close as I can realistically get to being the cowboy I wanted to be as a boy.

Music matters to me. I sometimes wish that comedy shows were more like rock gigs. Fans like it when bands go out and play classic albums in full, or do greatest hits tours, but comedians, with few exceptions, simply can't go out and just do their old stuff. I'd love it if I could just stroll on stage and start an old joke, and then point the microphone at the audience and let them finish it for me. I could say, 'Yeah! Thank you!' then go crowd-surfing while they all ask each other if they have got kids and where they come from. I think musicians have it easy in that respect – but how joyous to

---

* *I went on* Desert Island Discs *and I picked songs by the Beatles and Bowie and Simple Minds and Elvis Presley but I forgot all about ELO. I wish I'd picked 'Wild West Hero'. Then again, I suppose I might have started crying on Radio 4 in front of Kirsty Young, and that would have been awkward.*

have written a song that people love so much that they just want to hear it again and again and again.

At the same time, I can't pretend that I am a music fanatic compared to other people that I know. My sons, particularly Joe, educate me about new music, but as you grow older you get less and less inclined to turn into the next John Peel and obsessively seek out new stuff. I used to do a stand-up routine in which I confessed that I had bought an iPod that held 60,000 songs and I only owned six CDs.

As Seen on TV

I'm the same with TV. Nowadays, there is virtually zero chance that I will have seen the latest happening TV show that everyone is talking about. My family all got really into *Game of Thrones*, and I thought I would do the same because I saw it as a historical drama and I'm quite into the genre. But then a dragon came flying into a scene and I said, 'I'm sorry, that's NOT what I signed up for!' Now there is no chance I am ever going to watch it because it will take a lifetime to catch up. I just haven't got the commitment. A box set is like an affair. If you can get it over and done with in one night, so much the better.

Nor have I got time to try to get into television phenomena like *Love Island*. I have so much going on in my life at the minute that I hardly have time to write this book. I'm not going to give six weeks of my life to a bunch of kids in their twenties trying to get off with each other. I mean, even my agent is into *Love Island*, and the other day she was talking to me about it. She said: '*Oh my God, you should have heard the speech that one of the girls made! She had been with this guy and she was losing him, and she said, "I've got to leave – I can't stay. I found the love of my life and that love of my life doesn't love me back and the pain is too much and I've got to leave!" John, I was crying while I was watching it!'*

I asked her, 'How long has she known him for?'

And she said, 'Four weeks.'

Four weeks! I've been married for twenty-seven years – put me and Melanie on *Love Island*! Get people who have all been married for at least twenty-five years and put them on *Love Island*! It will be a completely different show when the sexual tension and the six-packs are replaced with the menopause, apathy and bad backs. *That's* a fucking telly programme!

I was talking to a senior executive at ITV about *Love Island* and he said it is an absolute phenomenon because it draws people in. Melanie says the same thing: she told me, 'Don't start watching it, because you won't be able to stop!' I suppose the weird thing about *Love Island* is that I've got an opinion about it and I've never even seen it. That's some power for a television programme – for you to have an opinion about something you don't know anything about (although, in the current political climate, this seems also to apply to most members of the Houses of Parliament).

To remain truly relevant, I would have to learn new skills, but … I'm middle-aged now. I'm not going to invest what time and ability I have left in trying to learn new things. My brain is chock-a-block as it is. My head is full of stuff that I already know and I can't un-know, and I still have to find room for the necessary new stuff. I still know how to load a VHS video recorder. That knowledge will never be useful to me ever again, but it occupies a small corner of my brain and thus is not allowing me to learn something new.

This all means that I've got to be selective about some of the new stuff that I'm told I need to know – because, let's face it, some of it is not worth knowing. We have gone way beyond our needs for entertainment as human beings. There are so many options; so many TV channels. You just think, who the hell is watching all of those? And sometimes, actually, the answer is nobody. I'll give you a great example.

I used to do some work with UKTV. They own the W channel that I did my interview show on. I was getting a great reaction to it in that loads of people were coming up to me and saying they liked it, even more than for big shows I had done on the BBC that had got four or five million viewers. But the viewing figures I was getting back from W didn't match the response I was getting. So, I asked them, what was going on?

A guy from UKTV explained it all to me. He said that viewing figures are calculated via 5,000 or so boxes that are scattered around the country, which is really not very many at all. The boxes send back the information on who is watching what to the TV bosses and they look at the age and demographic of the people who are watching that box, assume that they are representative of their demographic all over the country, and multiply these people by a certain factor to find a likely overall national viewing figure.

UKTV also have a channel called Eden, which is a nature channel. All of a sudden, its viewing figures totally fell off a cliff. They had completely vanished off the radar. Eden had always had a modest trickle of viewers but now suddenly it seemed *nobody* was watching it. So UKTV got on to the people who collect and collate the viewing figures and said to them, 'This can't be right – you're suddenly telling us that nobody whatsoever is watching the channel! What's going on?'

The viewing-figure collection company drilled down into their figures and they found that their usual estimate of Eden's viewing figures of about 10,000 people was basically a multiple of ... one woman, who was watching it somewhere in the West Country. They got in touch with this woman and asked her, 'What happened? Have you stopped watching Eden?'

'I went on holiday for three weeks,' she told them.

'Oh, so you haven't stopped watching it, then?' they asked her.

'I never watch it!' she told them. 'I just have it on in my living-room for my dog.'

Eden's viewing figures had dropped through the floor, and some people at the channel were in danger of losing their jobs ... because a dog in the West Country had gone into kennels for three weeks while its owner went on holiday. That story just about sums up the precarious world of television.

In Pods We Trust

Some people don't watch television at all nowadays. They listen to podcasts. It seems like everybody and his dog (not the dog in the West Country who went into kennels) is doing a podcast nowadays. I was going to do one with one of my sons, because I thought the father-and-son dynamic would be good, but then he decided that he didn't want to do it, and I couldn't be arsed doing it on my own. I'm not entirely sure the world needs another one hosted by a white, heterosexual middle-aged man, because there are thousands of those. To be honest, I often suspect that it might be better if, instead of everybody making podcasts, people just actually had a chat now and then.

I like some podcasts, such as Russell Brand's, because I love Russell and his podcast makes me think a bit, and Jessie Ware, because I went on it and I love her and her mum (ah, another parent–child combo!). But a lot of others I will never listen to because I haven't got time. It's also strange to walk around with someone talking in your head, but that is still preferable to walking around listening to music on headphones, because that confuses me. It makes me feel as if I'm in a film. If I am walking around the streets of London listening to somebody playing a saxophone, I'm thinking, *Be on your toes, John, something is going to happen in a minute! There's a lot of tension building up!*

If young people aren't listening to podcasts, they are watching YouTube. My kids watch shows on YouTube by people who are properly famous and have got millions of subscribers, and I have literally no idea who they are. At my age, I am not going to pretend to be part of the YouTube generation. There again, I am not an old fart about the YouTube phenomenon – I genuinely think it's great. As somebody who still has to go through the pain of presenting to television commissioners, I think if somebody can bypass that whole painful process, make something in their bedroom and reach out directly to millions of viewers, good luck to them.

Let me digress for a minute. When I worked in the pharmaceutical industry, I used to have to write business plans and sales projections and set targets. That was my bread and butter. Everything was considered and quantified to ensure growth in the business, and where it appeared that growth was threatened, it was addressed and new strategies put in place. This was how my professional career was judged: on my ability to make the future match the projection I had outlined on my spreadsheet.

I cannot begin to imagine how many business plans I wrote and presented in my previous life. How many PowerPoint presentations I gave. How many times I stood side-on so I could both look at the chart on the screen and address the audience, using a pointer to highlight things on the screen to the room of people, half of whom I knew would be thinking of something else while feigning interest. Nowadays it would be a laser pointer, but back in the day we used an actual pointer, also known as a stick. It was essentially a pool cue without the felt bit at the end.

In one of my early presentations as a sales rep, I brought along some actual snooker chalk to chalk the end of my pointer with. That was an early lesson in finding out that something is not funny if people have seen dozens of other people do it before. It was a strange feeling to have to carry on using the pointer with blue chalk on the end, even though the joke had met with utter indifference from my audience, who then became irritated by the blue chalk marks I was leaving on the screen.

Since leaving the pharmaceutical world, I have never written another business plan, but a big part of me wishes that showbusiness operated in the same way. Ultimately, the final decision on what we see on our TV screens is in the hands of a small handful of people. I know dozens of talented people who, for one reason or another, have never managed to get the television presence their talent deserves, or any television presence at all.

I totally get the fickle nature of the business, but part of me would like sometimes to go back to my old life and give a PowerPoint presentation to a TV commissioning executive, assessing how my most recent television appearances rated against my previous projections. I can imagine myself presenting a graph showing which demographic, from which postcode, laughed at which jokes, and how we could use that data to extrapolate future opportunities to grow the market for laughter to other demographics and postcodes.

Even if you get in the room with the TV high-ups and they decide you're worth putting on the screen, you cannot take anything for granted. You can always fall out of favour, either with the audience or commissioning executives. You are constantly spinning plates and trying to make the right decisions about what projects to take on – trying to strike the balance between having a presence on television and not being on it so much that people get sick of the sight of you.

As I have grown older, I have realised more and more that performing stand-up on television can grow your audience and let people know who you are and what you do, but what they see on the screen will only ever be a tiny representation of what you do. It will never be the full deal. Like most live events, stand-up on television is only, at best, 60–70 per cent as good as it is live. Being in a room with someone on stage talking and making you laugh creates a unique connection between the performer and the audience which can't be replicated as you sit on the settee eating your TV dinner off your lap. What is said may be funny, but comedy works best in a dingy cellar bar – where it should always live – or in the major arenas it often inhabits today.

That is where the magic happens, and I say this as someone who is lucky enough to have experienced both sides. I have sat in the audience at comedy gigs and spat out my drink in reaction to someone being incredibly funny. I have also stood on a stage and caused the same reaction (no, not being spat at!). There are few things in life more joyous than making people laugh – especially by saying something that has just occurred to you, and that you have never said before.

With the best will in the world, television struggles to reproduce that magic. I always say to people that if they enjoy comedy on TV, they should go to comedy clubs and see it live. Going to a comedy night is rarely a wasted evening. Even if the acts are terrible, you still have an anecdote: 'We went to a comedy club last night and the acts were rubbish! I didn't laugh once all night. I could have done better myself!' is a better story to tell at work than 'I watched a professional comedian on TV last night and I found him quite amusing.'

If you take nothing else from reading this book, take the message that you should get out more and go to some live events, particularly comedy. As it is a book about growing old, there is every chance that, having chosen to read it, you are already on your way to being old. You may even be thinking, 'No, I have never been to a comedy club, and I not going to start now!' Well, if *that* is your attitude, I don't want to be rude but please put this book down and piss off, because nothing else in here is for you.

On the subject of comedy and getting old, on my last tour I was talking a lot about turning fifty. I did a thing where I'd say to the audience, 'Give me a cheer if you are fifty or over.' There would be this kind of half-hearted, muffled 'Yeah!' Then I'd say, 'Give me a cheer if you are under fifty,' and there would be a massive roar. It was the same every single night. And then I would tell the audience: *'Listen to that! Listen to the enthusiasm, the optimism, the sound of joy in the young people's voices! Whereas you, first group, you older ones, are all wondering what time this finishes, thinking that you need a wee, and worrying how you are going to get home!'* The joke only worked because every night the reaction was the same. Under 50s have no idea how lucky they are ...

As you get older, you start thinking about things like that. My kids will tell me they want to go to something, and the first things that I ask them are, 'Where it is? How are you going to get there, and how will you get back?' They say, 'Huh? What are you asking us these things for? We just want to see the gig!' And I say, 'Well, these are the things that you need to know!' I turn into a middle-aged logistics freak.

I am the same at my own gigs nowadays. There is no greater sense of satisfaction than when I play a big arena show, with all the trucks and the heavy-duty set-up, and I can have my car actually inside the arena. I can literally walk off the stage and into the back of my car and be out of the back door before the audience have got out of their seats. I am looking back at my own venue and thinking, *Ha! I beat my own traffic!* It's sad, but these things matter when you get to my age.

Speaking Up

As with most things in my life nowadays, Melanie is the main person who keeps me relevant. If it wasn't for her, I wonder if I would ever leave the house if I weren't on tour. She likes to see new films and so we used to go to the cinema quite a lot – that was always our date night. But the world has changed and now, like everybody else, we are more likely to stay home with a box set than go to the pictures.

That's good for me in a way because cinemas can drive me mad. They are where I am at my absolute grumpiest. I can't stand being in the cinema when people are eating or chatting or on their phones during the film. It irritates the bollocks off me. I couldn't begin to say the number of times I have told somebody, 'Oi! You! Shut up!' When I was younger, I probably wouldn't have done that. I would have just sighed and tutted to myself . . . but not any longer.

It may all be part of being a grumpy middle-aged man, but actually I am proud of the fact that I speak up now when I am annoyed. I like the fact that I am admitting to myself that these people piss me off, and I like the fact that I'm bold enough to say to them, 'Oi! You! You are pissing me off!' I suppose I figure, *what have I got to lose?* If they don't like me as a result, who cares? There is a freedom as you get older just to say whatever you think, particularly if you look too old for anyone to actually want to fight with you.

It's only human nature to want to stay at least slightly relevant as you grow older but you also realise that some things that you used to do just don't apply to you anymore. When I was younger, like everybody else I would go out clubbing and come in at some point the next morning. Today, I need a serious excuse to be still up after 10.30 at night and I am certainly not going to be at a rave giving it large, blowing a whistle and wearing a fluorescent yellow vest.

People talk about 'dad dancing' and I suppose it happens to all of us eventually. Even if some of us are in denial. I'm sorry to keep going on about Liverpool's Champions League victory (well, no, I'm not) but after the final in Madrid, I managed to get me, two of my sons, my brother, my nephew and a cousin into the team's hotel. The atmosphere was as you would imagine after you had just won the Champions League. Everyone was enjoying themselves, it was an amazing party to be at and then at one point my cousin, Carl, who is well into his forties, came up to me all excited and said 'John, I've just had a dance-off with Virgil van Dijk!'

'Carl, mate,' I said. 'I wasn't even there, and I think I know who won that one!' I mean, Beyoncé would probably struggle in a dance-off with Virgil van Dijk. The fact that Carl was trying to suggest that it might have been a draw struck me as a little far-fetched.

Staying hip and relevant is a lovely idea ... but not at any cost. Some new things are simply not worth learning about. I am never going to understand bitcoins, for example, and I just don't want to. One of my sons is quite into bitcoins. He was trying to explain it to me and it was like he was talking Swahili. His generation and mine have a totally different understanding of the cyberworld. His generation believes that if things exist in computer code, they exist. My generation believes that if you can't touch it, it doesn't. Bitcoin seem to me like one of those things that, if you buy into it, you think you never have to prove it just because you have faith in it. It's a bit like religion.

I was really pleased the other day when I read Warren Buffett, who is one of the greatest financial brains of our lifetime, saying that bitcoins are essentially worthless. Warren Buffett said: *'If I give you a cheque for one million dollars, you can cash it because I have one million dollars that you can take from me. Cyber-currency is a different thing. If you have a bitcoin, what is it? How does it exist? There is nothing actually behind the bitcoin system, and at some point, it will collapse.'*

I admit that I was very relieved to read this because it made me feel as if bitcoins were one less confusing modern thing to worry about. There again, Warren Buffett is eighty-nine now, so maybe even he doesn't understand things quite as well as he used to. Maybe he is sitting somewhere now, baffled, trying to get his iPad to work by turning it off and turning it on again, and Face-Timing his grandkids from his pocket.

Some new technology is a little more accessible. When I was on tour last, I took Alexa with me in the dressing room. We had her at home as well for a while, until somebody told me that the people who control Alexa can listen to every word you say. Not that that would be a big problem for me, because Alexa was pretty shit at understanding what I was saying.

I think Alexa may have had a very sheltered life and never been to Liverpool or heard a Scouse accent. I would ask her, 'Alexa, what is the weather like?' and she would give me a recipe for lasagne. So, I just gave up and started asking her questions like, 'Alexa, how big is my cock?'

The funny thing about that was that she had an answer prepared for it. She told me, 'I'd rather not answer that question.' This means that during the development process, Alexa's engineers must have said, 'Look, at some point, some wanker is bound to ask Alexa how big his cock is! We had better programme in an answer.'

I can just about handle Alexa, but sometimes the technology that is being heralded as progress seems more like science fiction. I am never going to understand 3D printers and I might as well admit that to myself now. I saw a feature on the TV news, and the man being interviewed said that he was using 3D printers to make prosthetic limbs. I was utterly baffled: what is going to come out of the printer, a papier-mâché arm? I am pretty sure I am never going to use a 3D printer to make myself a new arm, so I think I can forget about them.

I think that is the trick of reaching this ripe old age – to know what you are never going to do, and to not feel bad about it. I am never going to read James Joyce's *Ulysses* and I don't give a toss about that. Nowadays, if I start reading any book and I get ten pages in, and I'm thinking *this is hard work*, I put it down and I don't pick it up again.

I still can't play that piano, nor the guitar that is standing next to it and maybe, just maybe, it is time to accept that I never will. At this point in my life, I may be as good as I am ever going to be. Or maybe I'll surprise myself in years to come. Who knows? The point is that *I am fine either way.*

I may never learn to play the piano and I may never wear the totally hip latest trainers again but the latter fact is entirely as it should be. I am a bloke in his fifties. While the world is facing global warming, the NHS is near to collapse, the government is falling to pieces and the risk of developing cancer gets higher with every day I live, if I were still worrying about owning the latest trainers, I think I would need to have a major word with myself. Thankfully, I'm not.

The other day, I went with a few people to a nice vegetarian restaurant in London. I didn't know what half of the things on the menu were, so I asked the waiter, 'Can you bring me some vegan food, please?' The waiter wanted to run through the entire menu with me and to discuss everything, but said, 'Look, I don't want to be rude, but please just bring me some vegan food. As long as you manage not to kill anything while you are making it, it will be fine.' Basically, the menu was outside of my sphere of knowledge and I was fine about that. Twenty years ago, I might have felt self-conscious, or insecure in that situation, but I don't anymore.

What it all comes down to is that it's nice to be relevant, as it is to be popular, but as you get older, you're less bothered about either. Both professionally and personally, there will always be people who don't like me. There is nothing I can do about that, so it is not worth worrying about. There are some critics who will come to review my next tour, because they always do, and I can write their review for them now. I know exactly what they are going to write before I even know what I am going to say on tour because I know that they don't like me.

I do wonder what the point is of the same critics coming to tour after tour of mine in order to tell the world that, yep, they still think I'm no good. One guy came to see me and he wrote: 'I sat in the arena, surrounded by people giving a standing ovation to a show that I thought was, at best, average.' I just thought, *Well, at least you admitted that I got a standing ovation!*

As I have got more popular, and played bigger and bigger venues, the people who proclaim what is hip and relevant have decided that I am a mainstream comedian and that mainstream equals middle of the road, which for some reason is a negative term. That is fair enough as far as I am concerned. There are plenty of comedians out there trying to be edgy and shock people and that's just not me. If critics have decided that I'm middle of the road that is basically their problem.

What *did* make me laugh was that another reviewer came to one of my arena dates and wrote: 'John Bishop is extremely popular and extremely likeable but not many people would call him cool. He is the Status Quo of comedy.' When the review came out, my agent bought me an actual Status Quo tour jacket off eBay and posted it to me. I thought that was hilarious, because I really don't care about that kind of bad review anymore. Life is too short.

And, also, because Status Quo have had some decent songs. They didn't make my *Desert Islands Discs*, and they have never made me cry like ELO, but they are still relevant to themselves, and they will always be relevant to millions of people. And, whatever age I happen to be, if I can carry on Rocking All Over the World that will do for me.

9.

HOW TO END THIS BOOK

THIS IS NOT THE first time I have tried to write a conclusion to this book and it will be not the first time in the process of writing the book that I will think I have got it wrong when I send it to be edited. I called my mum and dad and asked them for their tips about growing old. My mum, who is seventy-seven, said, 'Why are you asking us? We're not old.' My dad, who is seventy-eight, said the main thing he would pass on is that you have to remain positive because there is always something around the corner. When I pressed my mum on what was the best thing about growing old, she said, 'We keep the doctors in a job.' I made the call on Face-Time, and they held the phone between the two of them so they could both see me but I could only see half of them which felt very apt, because whatever I am today, or ever will be, I will only ever be half of each of them.

The reality is that this book has become more autobiographical than it was originally meant to be. I thought I would research facts and funny stories about other people growing old, maybe adding a little bit of my own experience on top. I've done a little bit of that, but the emphasis has been far more personal than I intended.

I spoke to a friend recently and mentioned that I was writing a book. He asked if it was an updated autobiography, as he knew that I have already done one. When I explained that this isn't what it was meant to be, and it was more a book about growing old, he asked if I was putting myself in it. When I said, 'Yes,' he looked at me like I was stupid: 'John, what do you think an updated autobiography *is*? It's the same person telling stories, but a bit older.'

My mate also told me not to worry that this book has morphed into something else because he was told when he did a similar project that 75 per cent of the people who buy celebrity books buy them as gifts for other people, and 75 per cent of the recipients never actually read them. If this is true, and you're one of those to have reached this point in the book, I am grateful to you. I will still bank the sales of the others, but you mean significantly more because you gave me your time. If writing this book taught me anything, it is that time is the commodity that we can never exchange, upgrade or repeat. We have the time we have allotted to us, and how we choose to spend that allocation defines the life we live and the people we become.

When I am on stage, whatever narrative I am following always has to lead to a joke. With this book, what started out as a light-hearted look at growing old and my own attempts to avoid a mid-life crisis has allowed me to not always look for the silly or funny. It has allowed me to look for the honest. At times it has been difficult because, outside of these pages, or being on stage or television, I do have a life and that life does not always operate as I would wish.

Over the months before and during writing this book, I have experienced depression for the first time in my life. I could point to the fact that within the last year we have moved house three times, which is said to be one of the most stressful things anyone can do. We lost Eileen, my mother-in-law, suddenly: something that, as an only child, hit Melanie very badly, as we saw her every day. I miss her too because when you love the same person, as she and I both did with Melanie, and want to take care of them, you establish a unique bond which is only strengthened when grandchildren are thrown into the equation.

I could point to my sons having the same challenges faced by anyone trying to find their feet in the world, and feeling that I have should have more answers for them than I do. I could point to having a knee operation that has taken me significantly longer to recover from than I anticipated, illustrating to me that the body I occupy is not what it once was. It is the body of a man who has been here for fifty-two years and counting, a body that no longer bounces back from injury or assault but crawls to recovery instead. I could point to the fact that the operation occurred the week after I finished my most successful tour to date, which more than any previous tour has left me wondering if I will ever hit the balance between honesty and comedy as well again.

I could point to the fact that the show I loved doing most on television, the *In Conversation With* ... interview show, was deemed to have reached its natural conclusion, and so no more would be made. Despite having great things in the pipeline, as TV people say, I am not certain I will ever produce anything that I will be as proud of again. I could point to the fact that I have moved a four-hour drive away from my mum and dad as they enter the twilight years of their lives, arguably placing a greater burden on my brother and sisters, although none of them would ever see it that way. Or I could point to the fact that somebody asked me to write a book about growing old and thus made me look at my life now, when I possibly understand it less than I ever thought I would.

I am not trying to claim there is anything unique about me. From what I have read, this air of sadness is not uncommon in people at this point in their life. Women have to go through the menopause, which I have learnt a lot about with Melanie. I can only reiterate her opinion that if men suffered from the menopause, we would have a cure that would be both free and compulsory. We would have a National Menopause Recognition Day, which would be supported by the Premier League, and it would be the only day that players could take their shirts off to cool down without being booked.

I am not being flippant here. Melanie has told me about, as well as the hot flushes and other physical symptoms, the mood swings and impeding sense of doom that can descend. She says you feel your body is possessed, because you know you are being unreasonable but you can't help it. A woman going through the menopause is suffering something beyond her control and deserves empathy and understanding, because precious few women feel they can tell the world that they need a window open in a business meeting, or that they will be fine in five minutes when the tears have stopped.

Yet at least women have a name for what is happening to them. With men, such feelings are often written off as just a sign of old-age grumpiness that is to be expected. The idea seems to be that once you have had a few weekends building a model railway in your shed you will be OK. Now that my personal fog is lifting, I can see that it is more than that.

I sought professional help when I first felt I was depressed. It was immediately after my leg operation early in 2018. I was staying in a hotel in London so I could have post-op physiotherapy in the hope it would aid the long-term recovery. One night I found I could not stop crying. I was alone in a posh hotel, crying, without any understanding why. I contacted a friend who I knew had suffered from depression and he put me on to his psychiatrist. The psychiatrist came to see me the very next day. When I told him about my feelings on ending the tour, my impending house move, my leg operation and my sense of a lack of direction, he looked me in the eye and said: 'To be fair, if I were you, *I* would be depressed.'

He said that all of these concurrent circumstances, added to me having had a general anaesthetic forty-eight hours earlier, would be reasonable grounds to feel depressed. I felt reassured by this and did not see him again, but a few months later it all came back. I felt that some things I had always taken for granted were now overwhelming, and I felt incapable of doing what were very simple tasks without them feeling like a huge effort. I was waking up and not looking forward to the day and the potential that it held. I was tired and I was lost.

This time, I went to see a counsellor. He sat and listened to me as I complained about everyone and everything in my life for an hour. When I had finished, he thanked me for coming, led me out and closed the door behind me, wishing me luck as he did so. I stood there as the door closed and realised that, apart from 'Hello' when I had arrived, they were the only words that he had said to me for the whole session. I had basically arrived and dumped all of my problems in a big pile in the centre of his room, like a laundry basket of pain, and I was expecting him to give it all back to me washed and ironed. That was when I realised that talking is good – even writing this feels like it is doing me good – but you have to do your own laundry. Nobody else, no matter how qualified they are, will be able to affect your feelings as much as you can.

As I thought about who else I could discuss this with, it became obvious to me that someone who was older and who has passed through this phase in their life would make sense. It would also help if they were in showbusiness, because in that world some things that seem trivial, like how you feel when you end a tour, only make sense if you have experienced it, whereas to the rest of the world it can look needy and self-indulgent.

For example, I would list among my greatest regrets the fact that I left a TV show called *A League of Their Own* far too early. There were numerous reasons for my decision at the time. And whatever the merits of those reasons, my regrets are to do with missing the people. For weeks at a time, I was paid to spend time with people whom I regard as friends – namely James Corden, Freddie Flintoff and Jamie Redknapp – and do silly things with them. I am still friends with them now but for some reason, based on the advice I was receiving and everything else that was happening, it seemed to me a good idea to leave. It is only a TV show and it has certainly not affected my overall career, or the success of the show, but I walked away from spending time with people that I liked, and that is the most important thing in life. Spending the time we have with the right people and choosing not to do so for some perceived career benefit was stupid. However, carrying regrets too far would only have a negative impact. A friend of mine summed it up with an old Jewish saying: 'This too is for the best.' I like this saying, but we all know as we grow older there are inevitably going to be regrets that we have to deal with.

To list this decision as among the biggest regrets I have in life either illustrates how great the rest of my life is, or is a reflection of how being in showbusiness can affect your sense of reality. There does seem to be a great contingent of people within show-business who have dark times. Perhaps it's because the highs that you enjoy are so high that it is hard to come down and find a level that feels balanced, and that is why things like leaving a show too early are given a level of importance you would not attribute to any other job.

Whatever regrets I have had in my career or in my 'real' life have always been hugely outweighed by the things I have got right. When your life is so much better than you ever imagined and you still feel down then it is apparent something is missing, and you need to filter things out by talking to someone. Bearing all of that in mind, I looked at my list of friends in my phone and it was quickly apparent to whom I should talk.

The Parsons' Tale

Nicholas Parsons is the oldest person that I know. He is also an unlikely friend in that few people would have instinctively put the two of us together. Over the years that I did the Edinburgh Festival I became friends with Nicholas, because every year he would invite me on to his own live on-stage interview show.

I should probably put this into context. When I first started doing the Edinburgh Festival in the early 2000s, I was unknown and was hardly pulling any audience at all. Nicholas was such a superb scout for new talent. He would come to see a new comic's show, and if he enjoyed it and if liked you, then there was a chance you would get on his afternoon interview show. This was an opportunity for his audience to hear about you and because his show always sold out, it was an opportunity to get a dozen or so more bums on seats for your own.

Even at ninety-five years old Nicholas had arranged to go to the Edinburgh Festival again in 2019, but after three days and three shows up there he was admitted to hospital after a fall. He stayed in hospital in Edinburgh for a couple of weeks before being transferred down to Stoke Mandeville Hospital in Buckinghamshire. Many ninety-five-year-olds recuperating from illness would not be keen on visitors but I knew that Nicholas would be different. He has such a keen mind and is made out of incredibly strong stock.

I recall Nicholas once telling me that in his early twenties he fell seriously ill with TB. The following year, doctors first began to use penicillin to treat such infections and he made a full recovery. He had been training as an engineer, but after his recovery he followed his heart's desire and went into acting, because his illness had made him realise the precarious nature of life and how important it is to seize the day and try to be what you want to be. I was deeply impressed by his tenacious personality that enabled him to get better and go into showbusiness. But I was even more impressed by the fact that I was talking to somebody *who was even older than penicillin*.

There can be nobody more of his time because Nicholas was born the year after John Logie Baird invented the television: it is almost as if showbusiness was waiting for him to arrive. Nicholas's extraordinary career has lasted for more than seventy-five years and, like any showbusiness career, it has not been without its ups and downs. However, what has kept him going through all of that time is his amazing resilience, positivity and complete unfettered love for what he does, whether it has been being an actor, a comedian or a quiz-show host. From his youth through middle age into his senior years, he has remained a master of the crucial art of remaining young at heart.

Sitting by Nicholas Parsons's bed in Stoke Mandeville Hospital, it struck me that perhaps this is the secret to avoiding a mid-life crisis and making sense of getting old. The trick is to make sure that you are doing something that you absolutely love – which, crucially, Nicholas was not initially able to do …

Me: You've had an amazing career to date, Nicholas, but it didn't start as you wanted, did it?

Nicholas: No. When I left school, aged sixteen, in 1939, my parents asked me, 'What do you want to do?' I said, 'There is only one thing I've ever wanted to do — I want to be an actor.' And my father said, 'Don't be ridiculous! That's not a proper job!'

Me: What about your mum?

Nicholas: She thought the same! She loved going to the theatre and yet she thought everybody who worked in showbusiness was debase, debauch and degenerate, and I would finish up an alcoholic pervert in the gutter. I said, 'But, mother, you admire people like Laurence Olivier and Ralph Richardson! Do you think *they* are like that?' She said, 'No, and it's a pity they have to work with that sort of people!'

Me: Ha ha! So, what did you do?

Nicholas: My parents put me into engineering and I did five years as an apprentice in Clydebank to qualify as a mechanical engineer. Then I joined the Merchant Navy until I got TB. When I got better, my parents asked me again, 'What do you want to do now?' And I told them the same as before: 'I'm going to be an actor.' They said, 'But you're a qualified engineer!' And I said, 'I know — I did that to please you, and now I'm going to please myself!'

Me: And how did you get into showbusiness?

Nicholas: I got some understudying parts in London. Then I heard about a play in the West End that was looking for five young male leads and I went to the theatre manager and asked to audition. He was busy, so I sat for three days in his outer office until he got so fed up of me that he agreed to see me. I got the part.

Me: How did your career progress from there?

Nicholas: I joined a repertory company in Bromley, then became half of a comedy duo. We took off, did summer seasons here and toured America. I did three years with Benny Hill, then became a quiz-show host with *Sale of the Century* for thirteen years. And, of course, on Radio 4 there is *Just a Minute*.

Me: How long has *Just a Minute* been going for?

Nicholas: Fifty-two years. It's the longest-running game show in the history of radio or television.

Me: *Fifty-two years!* Amazing! Well, this is a book about getting old, Nicholas, so how have you survived for so long? Is there a secret to your success?

Nicholas: I think the key is that *I have never felt old in my head*. All through the years, I have just pushed and pushed and pushed. It's crucial that I was thwarted in what I wanted to do when I was young. It made me try so much harder.

Me: It's easy to get jaded as you hit middle age. Did that never happen to you?

Nicholas: Never! Whatever age I have been, I have always loved what I do. I didn't do it because I wanted to be a star or to get well-known — I did it because I loved it. I knew that I was in another world on stage — expressing myself and fulfilling some urge within me.

Me: Where does that urge come from?

Nicholas: It's impossible to say, isn't it, John? But it keeps you young — and I think you are the same as me. I remember the stories you told me of how when you were starting out, you would go and do stand-up and not even tell your wife you were doing it. Then she came and saw you and she was very impressed.

Me: And you saw me in those early years ...

Nicholas: Yes! I saw your early show at Edinburgh in 'the hut', as you called it. You only had about twelve people watching you but I thought you were very, very good, so I asked you, 'Would you come and guest in my show?' You did, and you were tremendous there too.

Me: That's very kind of you.

Nicholas: Not as kind as you, that time a year or so later that you saved my bacon!

Me: You mean when your guest hadn't shown up?

Nicholas: Yes! We were in Edinburgh again and I was about to do my show and my guest never showed up. I was in a frightful pickle. The audience from the show before mine were just leaving and I spotted you in the audience and said, 'John! Are you doing anything? I don't have a guest — will you help me?' And you said 'Yes' straight away.

Me: In this book, I'm trying to understand how to grow old and how to do it well. You are ninety-five now, Nicholas, yet you are still pushing yourself —

why do you do it? Why did you go to the Edinburgh Festival this year when you weren't feeling well?

Nicholas: Well, I've gone on stage many times before when I've not been feeling well and just pushed through it. They call it Dr Theatre. You get on stage, the adrenaline pumps and you can do it. You don't want to take a break.

Me: No, you don't. I've had that same thing with Melanie, where she's said to me, 'Why don't you take a break?' But whatever age you are, you don't want to take a break from something that you love doing. And you become a prisoner to the fact that you love it.

Nicholas: I hadn't thought of it like that. It's a good way of putting it.

Me: So, maybe the secret to growing old is to carry on doing what you love doing? If you had a life lesson for the people reading this book, Nicholas, would it be to follow your passion?

Nicholas: Absolutely! Follow it and take every opportunity you can to express it. Think of the things that are positive — I do, I am a very positive person. But I must admit that this fall and illness feel like a wake-up call for me.

Me: How do you mean?

Nicholas: Well, because I have never felt old, and I have been able to push myself and work and be successful in my nineties, it made me think I was indestructible. Well, I'm not! *People don't like thinking about age.* They just get older and think they can carry on forever, but I'm finally going to have to start thinking carefully about pacing myself and what I can do. Because, eventually, you have to give way to *Anno Domini*.

Me: But you don't have to *give in* to it. You just have to change gear.

Nicholas: Yes. You just have to change gear — and find if there is another gear that works.

Me: I've no doubt there is.

Nicholas: Yes. Oh, and when I'm out of here, you *must* come on *Just A Minute*!

Me: I'd love to. I just have to find a minute.

As I drove home from talking to Nicholas Parsons, I was glad I had gone to see him. Even though his body was obviously frailer than when I had last seen him, his mind was still as sharp and his insight was clear. As a young man, he had left a safe profession to take a chance and follow his passion. He just simply could not ignore what was inside of him. And now, at ninety-five, he was thinking of slowing down but still couldn't help inviting me onto the next series of his radio show. He was already looking ahead. His natural enthusiasm and optimism would not allow him to do anything else.

My visit did not teach me anything that I did not already know about Nicholas. I knew that despite his body suddenly feeling older, his wit and his desire to do new things would not have waned. However, it did teach me something about me. Somewhere in the fog of my recent depression, I had lost a sense of what was important.

I am lucky enough to still have both of my parents alive. I have a brother and two sisters whom I am close to. I have mates whom I have known for decades, and who would still be my mates if I decided to give all of this up. For them, I am not defined by what I do but who I am, and who I have been. I am still married to the girl who took my breath away in a polytechnic library in 1988 and who can still do that now.

Marriage can be hard but, on a wet Wednesday, when you are watching a box set and saying nothing while a dog is trying to climb on the couch between you, I don't always express how grateful I am that I am sharing that experience with someone who knows me more than anyone. Melanie is the only person who saw me at the lowest points of my recent depression and she knows me inside out. For all my failings – of which there are many, as she knows – I would be a lesser man without her.

I have three sons making their way in the world and following their passions. I talk with them constantly and I am proud to be their father. They have faced many things but they are becoming good men and nobody can ask more than that. I have so many great things in my life that I could never have dreamt of. I am sure that from the outside it all looks perfect, and yet for a while, something had felt disjointed inside of me. Maybe what Nicholas had said had given me the answer.

I stopped my car, made a phone call, and changed direction.

The Bill Murray pub in Islington, north London, is the regular venue for the Angel Comedy Club. I had never gigged there but I had heard that it was a good room. It holds a maximum of seventy-five people and when I made an impulsive detour between Stoke Mandeville Hospital and home and arrived there, there were maybe forty-five there. It was an open mic night of the kind I used to play, back in the day. The punters don't actually pay, they just wander in, buy a pint and sit down to listen to whichever comedian happens to be on stage.

On my way home, I had phoned the club to ask if I could turn up and just do a short spot, for free, to whatever audience happened to be there. I arrived, and watched the first act from the back of the room, which was painted all black to give it that sense of intimacy that can make a comedy club feel like you are taking part in some secret meeting. Then the compère introduced me and I walked from the darkness through the small room, past some very surprised-looking people, and stepped onto the tiny stage. It was probably no more than four feet square, and the toes of the audience members in the first row were touching it. The lights were in my eyes.

I took the microphone from the stand, and I said something that was both a joke and a statement of truth in so many ways:

'I know! I can't believe I am here, either!'

The audience laughed.

I was home.

ACKNOWLEDGEMENTS

I WOULD LIKE TO acknowledge the support given to me during the writing of this book from Ian Gittins, who has helped me to come up with the structure of the themes; Andrew Goodfellow from Random House for suggesting I write the book and Anna Mrowiec for helping get it over the line.

I would like to thank Lisa Thomas for her continued support as my agent and my friend. I have to thank Melanie, Joe, Luke and Daniel for giving me a reason for everything I do.

I would like to thank those who have contributed by giving me their time and thoughts, including my mum and dad, Dylan Jones, Nicholas Parsons, Jimmy Gorst, the Lads and Melanie whose counsel I value above all others.

I have to thank the doctors and nurses of the NHS because, fundamentally, without them there would be no book about growing old, because it is only through them that I am here to write it. I would also like to thank the teachers who taught me as I grew up, when I was less willing to learn. I have never had the opportunity to thank them but I do so here because theirs is the profession I regard in the highest esteem; their work shapes the world of the future and I would be a very different person had I not had good teachers.

I finally have to thank Bilko, a fifteen-year-old deaf English bull terrier we found in a dogs' home fourteen years ago. He is a loyal friend and whatever room I have sat in to work on this book he has found his way there to lie at my feet throughout. I have many friends but he is the only one I know who would do that.

The advice on pages 144–157 from the fantastic NHS can be found here:

https://www.england.nhs.uk/wp-content/uploads/2019/04/
a-practical-guide-to-healthy-ageing.pdf

https://www.nhs.uk/live-well/healthy-body/

https://www.england.nhs.uk/wp-content/uploads/2019/04/
a-practical-guide-to-healthy-ageing.pdf

https://www.nhs.uk/live-well/healthy-body/eye-health-tips-for-
older-people/

https://www.nhs.uk/live-well/healthy-body/top-10-tips-to-
help-protect-your-hearing/

https://www.nhs.uk/live-well/healthy-body/look-after-your-
skin/

https://www.nhs.uk/live-well/sexual-health/sex-as-you-get-
older/